A question of evidence? Investigating and prosecuting rape in the 1990s

by
Jessica Harris and
Sharon Grace

A Research, Development and Statistics Directorate Report

London: Home Office

Home Office Research Studies

The Home Office Research Studies are reports on research undertaken by or on behalf of the Home Office. They cover the range of subjects for which the Home Secretary has responsibility. Titles in the series are listed at the back of this report (copies are available from the address on the back cover). Other publications produced by the Research, Development and Statistics Directorate include Research Findings, the Research Bulletin, Statistical Bulletins and Statistical Papers.

The Research, Development and Statistics Directorate

RDS is part of the Home Office. The Home Office's purpose is to build a safe, just and tolerant society in which the rights and responsibilities of individuals, families and communities are properly balanced and the protection and security of the public **RDS** are maintained.

RDS is also a part of the Government Statistical Service (GSS). One of the GSS aims is to inform Parliament and the citizen about the state of the nation and provide a window on the work and performance of government, allowing the impact of government policies and actions to be assessed.

Therefore -

Research Development and Statistics Directorate exists to improve policy making, decision taking and practice in support of the Home Office purpose and aims, to provide the public and Parliament with information necessary for informed debate and to publish information for future use.

First published 1999

Application for reproduction should be made to the Information and Publications Group, Room 201, Home Office, 50 Queen Anne's Gate, London SW1H 9AT.

Foreword

With one-quarter of recorded rape cases in England and Wales reaching conviction in 1985 and only one in ten in 1996, there is ongoing concern as to why the conviction rate is so low. The research outlined in this report was designed to examine this issue and identify the characteristics of those cases that reached conviction and those that did not. It was also intended to provide a comparison with previous similar Home Office research based on 1985 data. The most striking finding is that the nature of recorded rape cases has changed over the years. A far higher proportion now involves assailants known to the complainant (often including 'date rapes'). These types of case raise evidential difficulties and this has implications for the way they are dealt with by the criminal justice system.

David Moxon
Head of Crime and Criminal Justice Unit
Research, Development and Statistics Directorate.

Acknowledgements

We are very grateful to the Chief Constables and Chief Crown Prosecutors who agreed to take part in this study and, in particular, those in the five areas who helped us with our research.

Particular thanks are due to our liaison officers in each of the police forces' who were very helpful and co-operative, as well as to our contacts in the CPS. These people remain anonymous since we do not wish to identify the areas involved.

We are indebted to all those who agreed to be interviewed for this study, including judges, barristers, CPS lawyers and caseworkers, and the police, and particularly to the complainants who agreed to talk to us about their experiences.

Thanks are also due to the Saint Mary's Centre in Manchester for its important help and advice throughout the research. Jennifer Temkin and Sue Lees also provided helpful insights into some of the problems with rape cases.

Finally, we would like to thank our colleagues within RDS – David Brown for his extremely helpful advice and comments throughout the project, Pat Dowdeswell for her help and support with statistics, Robert Street for his assistance with interviews and drafting comments and Joel Miller for his invaluable help with the multivariate analyses.

Jessica Harris
Sharon Grace

Contents

List of tables

List of figures

Summary and recommendations

Background

There has been considerable concern in recent years about the continuing fall in the conviction rate for rape. In 1985 it stood at 24 per cent nationally but in 1997 was just nine per cent. The decline has occurred despite a range of initiatives to improve the criminal justice system's response in rape cases. These include a circular to the police, designed to elicit a more general sympathetic response to rape victims' and a change in the law to recognise that rape can be committed within marriage. The research described in this report was as a response to the concerns and had two main aims:

- to discover what factors influence whether an initially recorded rape leads to a conviction for rape;

- whether such factors have changed in recent years and, if so, whether this calls for changes in guidance or procedures.

Methods

The study examined nearly 500 incidents initially recorded as rape by the police in 1996 and followed their progress through the criminal justice system. Information was extracted from police and Crown Prosecution Service (CPS) files, using the complainant's account of the incident as the basic source of information, supplemented by police, medical and witness statements. Interviews were also carried out with police, CPS lawyers, barristers, judges and complainants. Some comparisons were possible with an earlier study by the Home Office, which drew on 1985 rape cases.

The changing nature of rape cases

- Rapes committed by a person unknown to the victim ('stranger' rapes) formed only 12 per cent of the sample; those committed by acquaintances or intimates accounted for 45 per cent and 43 per cent of cases respectively.

- This illustrates a very marked change from the previous Home Office study, in which stranger rapes constituted 30 per cent of all cases.

- Because, nationally, the number of recorded rapes has risen threefold since 1985, this indicates that the actual number of recorded stranger rapes has not changed significantly, but that the number of recorded 'acquaintance' and 'intimate' rapes has increased substantially.

The attrition process

The study found that only 6 per cent of the cases originally recorded by the police as rape resulted in convictions for rape. This represents 9 per cent of crimed rapes which is a similar figure to that recorded in the national statistics (see Appendix A). Of the initial sample of cases:

- 25 per cent were no-crimed by the police;

- no suspect was identified in 11 per cent;

- the police took no further action (NFA) against the suspects in 31 per cent;

- 8 per cent were discontinued by the CPS;

- 7 per cent resulted in an acquittal or the case to lie on file;

- 7 per cent resulted in a conviction for an offence other than rape.

Relationship between complainant and suspect

- Cases involving acquaintances were most likely to be no-crimed.

- Cases involving intimates were most likely to be NFA-ed or discontinued by the CPS.

- In the minority of stranger rape cases where a suspect was identified, the case was more likely to proceed to court than in those cases where the complainant and suspect were previously acquainted.[1]

Detection

- Of cases which were crimed, only 15 per cent went undetected.

---

1   Nine stranger cases reached court.

- The detection rate in stranger rape cases was considerably lower than average: despite advancements in forensics, only one-third were detected.

Police decision-making

No-criming

Home Office guidance advises that the police may no-crime a case where the complainant 'retracts completely and admits to fabrication'.

- There appears to have been a reduction since 1985 in the proportion of cases no-crimed – from 45 per cent to 25 per cent.

- Although the most common reason for no-criming decisions was that the complaint was believed false or malicious, over one-third of cases were no-crimed because the complainant withdrew and 15 per cent because there was insufficient evidence.

- The strongest predictors of whether cases were no-crimed were the age of the complainant and whether violence was used during the attack. Thus, cases were least likely to be no-crimed where the complainant was aged under 13 or where violence was used during the assault.

No further action

- Half of all detected crimed cases were NFA-ed. In fact, a reduction in the no-criming rate appears to have been offset by an increase in the NFA rate.

- The most common reason for cases being lost here was complainant withdrawals – half were NFA-ed for this reason and one-third due to insufficient evidence.

- The strongest predictors of whether cases were NFA-ed were the age of the complainant, whether violence was used during the attack and the degree of consensual contact between the complainant and suspect prior to the attack. Thus, cases were most likely to proceed involving complainants under 13 where violence was used during the attack and there had been no prior contact between complainant and suspect.

- The police sought CPS advice in 20 per cent of detected cases – mostly because of evidential problems. The CPS usually confirmed police concerns over evidential sufficiency and advised no further action. It transpired from interviews with prosecutors that they would like to see more advice cases.

CPS decision-making

- Half of all cases were crimed and detected by the police and sent to the CPS for a decision on prosecution. The CPS discontinued just over a quarter of these cases.

- It is rarely in the public interest to discontinue a case of rape. Of the cases that the CPS discontinued, only 15 per cent were dropped on public interest grounds. These were non-stranger rapes where the complainant was unwilling to attend court and a witness summons to compel attendance was felt inappropriate. All the other cases discontinued were dropped on evidential grounds.

- There was found to be a significant association between the age of a complainant and whether a case was discontinued – those involving particularly young or particularly old complainants were most likely to be proceeded with.

At court

- The nature of cases reaching court has changed over the last ten years or so – many more acquaintance and intimate cases means that the issue is increasingly one of consent.

- Two-thirds of defendants reaching the Crown Court were convicted of an offence. Just over one-quarter of defendants were convicted of rape or attempted rape.

- One-quarter of all Crown Court cases resulted in an acquittal, usually by a jury.

- Attrition occurred where three-quarters of defendants pleading guilty to lesser charges were convicted of those charges only, indicating a form of plea-bargaining between the prosecution and the defence.

- A number of those interviewed suggested that severe sentences in rape cases involving acquaintances or intimates – five-year starting point in contested trials – indicates that juries are reluctant to convict.

Discussion

Consideration should be given to re-issuing guidance on the no-criming of rape cases and ensuring that this is covered in police training and HMIC inspections.

There is a need:

- for improved levels of support for complainants at all stages;

- for improved levels of communication – between the police and the CPS, and between the police and complainants;

- for better evidence-gathering in the form of photographs and reports that can be used at later stages;

- for training and refresher training for all concerned;

- for measures to provide better protection for vulnerable or intimidated witnesses in rape trials;

- for an improvement in prosecution standards, ensuring that prosecuting barristers pay is broadly similar to that of defence lawyers, to remove possible imbalances;

- to address the issue of how rape is defined, including whether it should be 'graded' in some way (a Review of Sex Offences will be a useful opportunity to consider this).

Further research might examine how complainants are treated during the early stages of the process and provide a better understanding of why complainant withdrawals occur. Further work might also more thoroughly assess the reasons behind attrition and precisely how decisions are influenced at each stage. Also, in considering best models of practice, it is worth looking at how rape is processed in other countries (again, something that will be considered in the Sex Offences Review.)

Recommendations arising from the research

1. The existing guidance on restricting the circumstances in which cases may be no-crimed remains valid. Consideration should be given to its reissue, and to ensure that it is adequately covered in police training and in HMIC inspections.

2. Those reporting rape to the police should be given greater support, perhaps involving agencies other than the police. Some other jurisdictions (eg some US states) have involved victims more closely in the investigative process, and have coupled this with support to help them persevere. There are various models which would be worth more thorough investigation.

3. There is a particular problem with intimate and acquaintance rapes where there is a need to identify the specific reasons for cases being dropped which was not possible in the present study.

4. The police should be more disposed to consult the CPS in borderline cases, and should not be too quick to assume that cases that may look unpromising could not be built up, especially if the complainant can be drawn more prominently into the process.

5. It is interesting that cases in which there is evidence of violence are often dropped. There would appear to be scope for better evidence-gathering, eg through photographs and medical reports, and for ensuring that such evidence is given due weight in later discussions.

6. Individual police officers rarely deal with rape – the number of rapes reported each year is only about one-twentieth of the number of police officers. There is a clear need to cover in training the issues raised by rape cases, but also to ensure that refresher training is given as best practice develops.

7. Further research could examine the ways in which cases are dealt with and complainants treated in the early stages of the process in order to produce a better understanding of why withdrawals occur. This would more clearly identify the dynamics of the process, which was not wholly possible in the present study.

8. A comprehensive study, to include tracking cases in detail and interviewing decision-makers and complainants in specific cases, would identify both the reasons why the CPS drop cases and recommend the police not to charge. This would accord with the recommendation in the Glidewell Report that a study should be made of the reasons for discontinuance in more serious offences.

9. Although in the present study some lawyers expressed reservations about meeting victims, Glidewell offers the idea of meetings with the complainant as an idea worth discussion. The report 'Speaking Up For Justice' makes a recommendation (Recommendation 27) for meetings between the prosecutor and certain vulnerable or intimidated witnesses, claiming that it would assist the presentation

of the case and provide reassurance for the witness. It is worth considering the practices of other countries such as the USA, where the equivalent of the CPS does meet with complainants.

10. A study of those types of offence with a high rate of charge reduction, as recommended in the Glidewell report, would help identify the underlying reasons for the change in the nature of charges.

11. The Review of Sex Offences will provide a useful platform by which to consider whether there should be any changes in the way rape is defined, including whether it should be 'graded' in some way: the dichotomy between initial recording and conviction is clearly unsatisfactory. It runs counter to moves in the context of violent offences to settle charges at an early stage, generally to provide a firm base for later decision-making, for example in terms of early guilty pleas.

12. There is a need to improve standards of prosecution and to ensure that prosecuting barristers' pay is broadly similarly to that of defence lawyers (to remove possible imbalances in the level of expertise on each side).

13. Other points emerging from this research simply reinforce the cases for change already before Parliament, which are designed to give more protection to vulnerable victims and witnesses.

1. Introduction

Background to the research

Apart from murder, rape is perhaps the crime that horrifies most. Rape of a woman is legally defined as 'sexual intercourse where a man knows that a woman is not consenting or is reckless as to whether or not she is consenting'[2]. Young women fear rape above all other crimes (Hough, 1995) and may actively adapt their lifestyles in ways that aim to avoid the risk of being attacked (Hough, 1995; Stanko, 1990). Such concerns are reflected in (and some would say fuelled by) media reporting of rape cases. Over the past decade, in particular, such reporting has focused on what has been seen as the criminal justice system's 'failure' to achieve convictions in rape cases. Indeed, the criminal statistics do indicate a big drop in the conviction rate for rape cases since 1985 (see Appendix A).

This decrease in the conviction rate has occurred despite numerous policy and practice initiatives aimed at improving the criminal justice response to rape. For example, Home Office Circular 69/1986 encouraged the police to have a more sympathetic approach when dealing with rape victims, and this is thought to account for much of the increase in reporting and recording of such offences. Further, the House of Lords in *R v R (1997)*[3] upheld the Court of Appeal's decision that rape can be committed within marriage and this ruling was given statutory effect in the Criminal Justice and Public Order Act 1994. The 1993 Sexual Offences Act changed the law so that boys under the age of 14 could be charged with rape.

The Home Office has previously addressed the issue of attrition in rape cases. In 1992 a report was published that showed that only one-quarter of cases initially recorded by the police resulted in a conviction for rape in 1985 (Grace et al, 1992). The study identified three key points of attrition in the criminal justice process:

- when the police decided to no-crime the incident;

- when the police, having initially recorded the incident as a crime, decided not to proceed to prosecution;

---

2   Since 1985 the law has been changed – making it possible for rape to be perpetrated on a male, although this is not within the remit of the present study.

3.   R v R (1997) 4 AU ER 481, HL.

1

- when most of those who were convicted at court were not convicted of rape.

The study drew attention to the widely different circumstances in which rape occurs. It identified three main categories:

- 'Stranger' cases comprise those where the suspect had had no contact with the complainant prior to the attack.

- 'Acquaintance' cases were those where the complainant and suspect were casually known to one another, eg the complainant had accepted a lift from the suspect, they had a prostitute and client relationship or they had met at a party.

- 'Intimates' covered those where the suspect was having, or had had, a relationship with the complainant, was a friend or was a member of her family – such cases often involving children. There were 22 cases of marital rape.

These differences have important implications for the likelihood of offenders being successfully prosecuted and convicted. The previous study found that those cases that typically resulted in a conviction for rape involved young, single women attacked by strangers who were also physically injured in the attack. Alleged attacks by acquaintances were:

- the *most* likely to involve the withdrawal of the complaint;

- the *most* likely to be contested;

- the *least* likely to result in a conviction.

The 1985 figures provide a benchmark for assessing change, both in the types of case coming to police attention and in the way the criminal justice system responds.

Aims of the research

This study had two key aims:

- to discover what factors influence whether an initially recorded rape leads to a conviction for rape; and

- whether such factors have changed in recent years, which might in turn call for changes in guidance or procedures.

The research also addressed:

● whether there have been changes in the types of rape case coming to police attention – as between rapes involving strangers, acquaintances and intimates;

● if so, did this change contribute to the reduction in the proportion of reported rapes resulting in conviction, and, if it did, was this due to evidential difficulties with acquaintance rapes or to other factors?

● what kind of cases are most likely to be discontinued by the CPS and why? Do cases where the defence of consent was used 'fail' at a greater rate than others?

Methodology

Using police and CPS files, the study traced the progress of 483 cases initially recorded as rape in 1996 and extracted details about the characteristics of each case. The statement of the complainant was used as the main source of information, backed up by the police, witness and medical examiners' statements. The sample was drawn more or less equally from five police force and CPS areas, representing metropolitan, urban and rural areas. Male rape cases were not included: they would raise different issues, are comparatively rare and would need to be studied separately[4].

The 483 rapes were reported by 456 complainants, indicating that some complainants reported more than one rape. The tables are based mainly on all 483 rapes.

In addition to the main quantitative study, a total of four focus group meetings were held with the police and the CPS. The police representatives specialised in dealing with rape cases. The CPS focus groups comprised both lawyers and caseworkers. Using vignettes of cases as a starting point for a free-ranging discussion, respondents were asked about their experiences in dealing with rape cases and for their views on the difficulties investigating, charging and prosecuting such cases.

Individual interviews were held with five judges experienced in dealing with rapes and with five barristers. Seven trials were observed at the Old Bailey. Finally, a small sample of self-selected women who withdrew their allegations during the police investigation were interviewed to discover the reasons behind their decision not to proceed. These women were not from the complainant sample for this study. Withdrawal from the case by the

---

4   Recently reported efforts by the Metropolitan Police Service confirm the different issues and taboos in dealing with male rape (*The Guardian*, 3 Mar 1999).

complainant was by far the most common cause of cases being dropped. Although only four women, contacted through a centre which deals with rape complainants on a day-to-day basis, agreed to take part, their experiences were of interest and chimed with other research (see Appendix E).

2. The sample

The changing nature of rape cases, 1985-1996

There is a striking difference in the nature of initially recorded rapes between the previous study (Grace et al, 1992) and this study. The proportion of all rape cases categorised as stranger rapes dropped from 30 per cent in 1985 to 12 per cent in 1996. The total number of recorded rape offences has increased more than threefold, so the number of *stranger* rapes has not changed significantly between the two studies. By contrast, the number of acquaintance and intimate rapes has increased greatly. To illustrate this point, Figure 2.1 shows the national total of crimed recorded rapes and projects the breakdown of the three types of rape from the two Home Office studies thereon.

Figure 2.1: **Estimated breakdown of types of rape cases, 1985 and 1996**

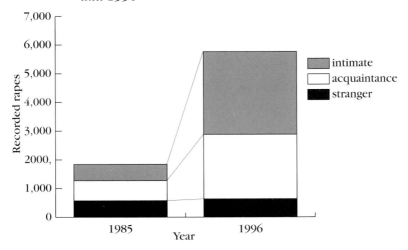

Relationship between complainant and suspect

Table 2.1 gives a more detailed breakdown of the relationship between complainant and suspect for cases in the present study.

Table 2.1: Relationship between complainant and suspect – reported rapes

	per cent	n=
Strangers	**12**	**(52)**
Acquaintances	**45**	**(194)**
Met within 24 hours		(102)
Met more than 24 hours before		(70)
Known vaguely		(12)
Prostitute and client		(10)
Intimates	**43**	**(204)**
Relative (not father)		(10)
Parental figure		(32)
Current husband		(22)
Former husband		(8)
Current co-habitee		(2)
Former co-habitee		(1)
Current boyfriend		(40)
Former boyfriend		(44)
Work colleague		(3)
Friend		(34)
Family friend		(8)
TOTAL	100	(450)

Note: n=450 of 483 initially recorded rapes for which relationship is known

Table 2.2: Marital status of complainant

	Stranger %	Acquaintance %	Intimate %	All %
Single	55	74	61	66
Cohabiting/long-term relationship	19	12	18	16
Married	14	8	9	9
Separated	5	2	7	5
Divorced	7	4	4	4
Widowed	-	1	1	1
TOTAL (n)	100 (42)	100 (167)	100 (193)	100 (402)

Notes:
1. n=402 of 483 initially recorded rapes for which complainant's marital status and relationship were known.
2. Percentages do not always add up to 100 due to rounding.

Table 2.2 shows that over three-quarters of complainants were either single or no longer in a relationship. In one-third of cases where the complainant was in a relationship, the allegation was against their partner.

Table 2.3: *Age of complainant by complainant/suspect relationship*

	12 and under	13-15	16-25	26-35	36-45	Over 45	TOTAL (n)
Stranger %	3	12	11	15	9	21	12 (52)
Acquaintance[5] %	30	52	46	34	51	25	43 (191)
Intimate %	67	37	43	52	40	54	45 (203)
Total % (n)	100 (33)	100 (87)	100 (164)	100 (95)	100 (43)	100 (24)	100 (446)

Notes:
1. n=446 of 483 initially recorded rapes for which age of complainant and complainant/suspect relationship were known.
2. Percentages do not always add up to 100 due to rounding.

The age make-up of the complainant sample was similar to that of the previous Home Office study (Grace et al, 1992), although slightly more complainants (just over one-quarter) were under 16. Most of the remainder (58 per cent of the total) were aged 16 to 35. Only 5 per cent were over 45.

- Complainants under the age of 12 were the most likely of the age categories to have reported being raped by someone they knew well and least likely to have been raped by a stranger.

- Complainants between 13 and 15 years of age were the most likely to have reported being raped by an acquaintance.

- Complainants over the age of 45 were the most likely to have reported being raped by a stranger.

Although data was collected on ethnicity, detailed analysis was not possible due to the small numbers on which this information was available.

---

5   A large proportion of girls under 16 were raped by acquaintances, often within 24 hours of first meeting them. One-quarter of suspects in these cases were also under 16 and just over one-quarter between 16 and 25. They usually met at a public outdoor place and attacks were likely to take place in either the suspect's home (30%) or some other private indoor place (26%).

Circumstances surrounding the attack

Consensual contact

Table 2.4:   Degree of consensual contact prior to rape

	Stranger %	Acquaintance %	Intimate %	All %
Had sexual intercourse with suspect	-	3	4	3
Had sexual contact (not intercourse)	-	3	4	3
Had prior sexual relationship with suspect		1	48	23
Voluntarily kissed with suspect	-	10	5	7
Allowed suspect to put his arm around her		2	1	1
Accepted invitation into suspect's house	-	17	6	10
Accepted a lift with suspect	-	17	2	8
Walked home with suspect	-	4	1	2
Danced with suspect	-	3	-	1
Case of child abuse[6]	-	-	16	7
Other	-	29	11	18
No consensual contact immediately prior to attack	100	10	4[7]	18
TOTAL (n)	100 (47)	100 (174)	100 (197)	100 (427)

Notes:
1. n=418 of 483 initially recorded rapes for which consensual contact and relationship were known; consensual contact was known for 427 in total.
2. Percentages do not always add up to 100 due to rounding.
3. 'Other' covers a range of circumstances: for example, where the complainant woke up in the suspect's bed, she gave him directions or he showed her round a house.

In 82 per cent of cases, there was some degree of consensual contact between the complainant and suspect immediately prior to the attack. This compares with the previous Home Office study (Grace et al, 1992) in which there was prior consensual contact in 37 per cent of cases. The differences between the two studies will partly reflect the growth in the proportion of acquaintance/intimate rapes. Almost one-quarter of complainants had had a prior sexual relationship with the suspect – as against three per cent in the previous study. All cases of child abuse involved intimate relationships, usually involving a parental figure. In many cases involving acquaintances, the complainant went back home with the suspect, having met him at a public venue, as reflected in their accepting a lift from, or an invitation to the home of, the suspect.

---

6   Degree of consensual contact in this context is a proxy for some form of intra-familial relationship, which is involved in most child abuse cases.

7   Consensual contact was the degree of contact immediately prior to the attack and therefore was recorded as none if, for instance, a complainant awoke to find the suspect in her bedroom, which might involve intimates.

Location of attack

Table 2.5: Location of first offence

	Stranger %	Acquaintance %	Intimate %	All %
Workplace	-	-	1	<1
Home of victim	6	16	32	22
Home of suspect	-	26	24	22
Home of complainant and suspect	-	1	30	13
Other indoor/private place	14	24	7	16
Park/green site in town or built-up area	14	3	2	4
Field/countryside	2	-	-	<1
Suspect's car	2	14	2	7
Complainant's car	-	1	1	<1
Public area	55	14	2	13
Waste ground	4	1	-	1
Other	4	1	1	1
TOTAL (n)	100 (51)	100 (185)	100 (199)	100 (462)

Notes:
1. n=435 of 483 initially recorded rapes for which location of attack and relationship were known; location was known for 462 in total.
2. Percentages do not always add up to 100 due to rounding.
3. Including alleyway, street area, railway station, bus stop.
4. Including building sites, rubbish dumps, disused areas of land.

Almost three-quarters (73%) of alleged offences took place in a private setting. Cases of child abuse involving intimates invariably took place at a private indoor place which was usually the home of the complainant and/or suspect. Only 18 per cent of alleged attacks occurred outdoors, with a further seven per cent taking place in the suspect's car. These findings are similar to those of the previous study (Grace et al, 1992), although more complainants were found to go back to the *suspect's* home in the present study.

3. The processing of rape cases by the police

This chapter examines the factors which influence the processing of rape cases – from the decision on whether to record the allegation as a crime to the decision on whether to charge.

In the past, a common defence in rape cases was that the suspect had been wrongly identified. In stranger rape cases the police investigation will aim to identify the suspect – perhaps through an ID parade or even Crime-Stoppers appeals to the public. In addition, with the development of forensic testing and DNA profiling in particular, it is now usually possible to prove (if the rape is reported promptly) that intercourse has occurred and the identity of the assailant.

Evidence is especially problematic in cases where:

- a complainant and suspect are known to one another;

- there was some degree of consensual contact leading up to the alleged attack; and

- there is little evidence of any violence or injury (Grace et al, 1992; Wright, 1984; Chambers and Millar, 1986; Lees and Gregory, 1993).

Overview of police decision-making

Once an allegation of rape has been made to the police, there are circumstances in which the case can subsequently be 'no-crimed'. If the police do decide to treat the case as a crime, they may nevertheless decide not to pursue it if they feel the chances of a successful prosecution are slight. The relationship between a complainant and suspect had a strong bearing on the attrition process, as Table 3.1 shows.

Table 3.1: *Attrition prior to first court appearance according to relationship between complainant and suspect.*

	Stranger %	Acquaintance %	Intimate %	All %
No-crimed	28	30	16	25
Undetected	48	13	2	11
No further action	4	24	45	31
Cautioned	-	1	1	1
Charged	20	32	36	31
TOTAL (n)	100 (52)	100 (194)	100 (204)	100 (483)

Note:
1. n=450 of 483 initially recorded rapes for which both relationship and outcome prior to court were known.
2. Percentages do not always add up to 100 due to rounding.

Table 3.1 shows that no-crime rates for alleged stranger and acquaintance attacks were quite similar – close to 30 per cent, compared with 16 per cent of cases involving intimates. The latter were therefore more likely to be crimed but were also more likely to result in no further action.

Table 3.2 provides more details of the relationship between police decision-making and the nature of the case.

Table 3.2: *Association between circumstances of the allegation and police decision-making*

	No-crime (n=124) %	(n)	No further action (n=151) %	(n)
Relationship				
Stranger	28	(14)	15	(2)
Acquaintance	30	(59)	43	(47)
Intimate	16	(33)	55	(92)
Age of complainant				
12 and under	6	(2)	27	(8)
13-15	23	(22)	28	(18)
16–25	26	(46)	51	(55)
26–35	29	(29)	75	(41)
36–45	35	(17)	77	(20)
Over 45	28	(7)	56	(9)
Degree of consensual contact				
Some	22	(78)	50	(124)
None	23	(17)	27	(9)
Use of violence				
Some	15	(37)	43	(76)
None	23	(20)	54	(33)

Notes:
1. No-crimes: the per centage refer to the number of initially recorded rapes. No further actions: the per centage refer to the number of crimed and detected rapes.
2. All associations were significant at the 99 per cent level.

Multivariate analyses showed that violence and age were found to predict no-criming decisions and violence, age and consensual contact were found to predict the police taking no further action (see Appendix D).

Salient points from Table 3.2 are as follows.

● No-criming is least likely with intimate rapes, victims aged under 13 and where violence has been used.

● Cases where there was no evidence of any violence or the threat of violence towards the complainant were more likely to be no-crimed. The most common reason for this was retraction by the complainant. In contrast, evidence of injury could both strengthen a case in the eyes of the police and make the complainant more determined to persevere.

● No further action is most common with intimate rapes, where complainants are aged between 26 and 45 and where there has been some consensual contact.

● Over half of those cases where there was no evidence of any violence or injury to the complainant were NFA-ed. When controlling for other factors, the lack of evidence of violence by a suspect was one of the strongest predictors of cases being no-crimed or NFA-ed.

Figure 3.1 indicates the different reasons for police decisions to no-crime and NFA.

Figure 3.1: Reasons given for no-criming and no further action by the police

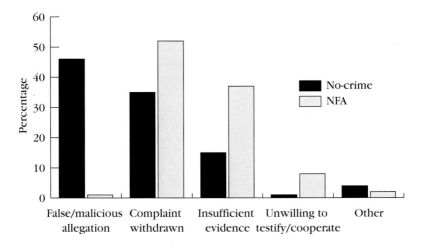

The main reason for cases not proceeding to a charge was withdrawal by the complainant – more than half the cases were NFA-ed for this reason. Thirty seven per cent of cases were NFA-ed on the grounds that there was insufficient evidence to proceed.

Of course, the police effectively have little choice when a complainant withdraws (although they may influence that decision). Cases where the complainant withdraws tend to be those where there is a high degree of consensual contact, and even where the complainant does not withdraw the chances that the case would succeed in court are often relatively poor.

The key issues of no-criming and whether to take further action are considered in more detail below.

No-criming

Although one-quarter of all cases were no-crimed[8], the level is much lower than previously. In a study based on 1985 data, Lloyd and Walmsley (1989) found that the average no-criming rate during the second quarter of 1985 was 45 per cent (though ranging from nil to 86 per cent between forces). The fall is consistent with guidance given to the police in Home Office Circular 69/1986, which states that no-criming is only appropriate where 'the complainant retracts completely and admits to fabrication'. However, there was variation between forces in the study, from 14 per cent to 41 per cent, and Table 3.3 shows that reasons for no-criming were not confined to complaints being false.

Table 3.3: **Reasons given for no-criming according to relationship between complainant and suspect**

	Stranger %	Acquaintance %	Intimate %	All %
Complaint withdrawn	14	42	33	36
False/malicious complaint	64	37	52	43
Insufficient evidence	21	15	12	15
Unwilling to testify	-	-	3	1
Other	-	5		5
TOTAL (n)	100 (14)	100 (59)	100 (33)	100 (123)

Note: n=106 of 483 initially recorded rape cases for which both relationship and reasons for no-criming were known.

Although the most important single reason for the police deciding to no-crime a case of rape was that the complaint was false or malicious, many cases were dropped for evidential reasons or because the complainant withdrew.

---

8   This figure was an estimate based on the 1985 data also used in the previous rape study (Grace et al, 1992). See Appendix B for more information on the bases on which the two rape studies are compared.

While a single reason for no-criming was usually recorded on the police file, in practice there might be several reasons. For example, the main reason might have been that a complainant withdrew her allegation, although it was clear from the file that in some cases the police also suspected the allegation to be false or thought the evidence was weak.

Detection

In 15 per cent of crimed rapes no suspect was caught. This was so in 66 per cent of stranger cases, compared with 17 per cent of acquaintance attacks and only three per cent of incidents involving intimates. Forensic testing was used in 108 crimed cases – taking the form of DNA profiling in just over half of these. In three of the 13 stranger rape cases, forensic testing established identity. However, it appears that detection rates for stranger rapes are poor despite advancements in forensics including DNA profiling – (of crimed cases, two-thirds of stranger rapes were undetected in the present study compared with one-third in the previous study (Grace et al, 1992))

Once detected, attacks by strangers were the least likely to be NFA-ed. However, the relatively low detection rate for these cases means that, in practice, they are the least likely to be prosecuted.

No further action

In considering further progress of cases through the system it is helpful to discard the 25 per cent of cases which were no-crimed and focus on those that survived this initial filter. The characteristics of the crimed sample are described in Appendix C. Figure 3.2 shows what happened to these cases.

Perhaps the most striking feature of Figure 3.2 is that it shows that half of all crimed cases that were counted as detected resulted in no further action.

For practical purposes, cases are still being lost since a reduction in no-criming might be largely offset by an increase in NFA cases. Such a shift might therefore have symbolic importance, and police sometimes showed a keen awareness of this:

> "If rape was treated as any other crime you would probably no-crime a lot more. But because rape is treated as something special, and indeed it is a serious crime, it is much more difficult to no-crime it."

The impact of Home Office guidelines comes through in the following note, written by a detective superintendent to whom the file had been submitted suggesting a no-crime:

> *"I am concerned to note that this allegation has been classified 'no-crime' – this classification is contrary to service policy... the victim expressed a desire that police did not pursue the allegation of rape. She does not state that the offence did not take place... the allegation must be classified as a rape."*

This case was, indeed, recorded as a crime although the police subsequently took no further action.

Incidents involving acquaintances normally involved some degree of consensual contact between the complainant and suspect prior to the attack. More than three-quarters of these cases involved complainants and suspects who had met within 24 hours of the attack – which would cover most of what are commonly described as 'date rapes'. Fifty-one per cent of acquaintance cases where there had been some prior consensual contact were NFA-ed, compared with half this number where there had been none.

Police interviews confirmed that evidence of a complainant having consented to being with a suspect, having perhaps left a club with him and having not sustained injuries, would tend to undermine her case:

> *"... people would think there are no visible injuries to her... they had both been drinking... had an evening together and she left with him quite happily, got into his car, went back to his flat...that dirt gets thrown up."*

Figure 3.2: Flow diagram illustrating the attrition process of rape cases (percentages)

(base = overall sample of crimed cases, n=360)[9]

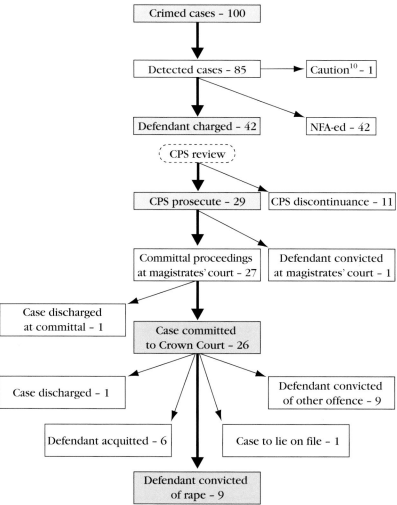

Case characteristics and police decision

Group attacks

Twenty-seven cases involved group rapes with two or more suspects: the majority of these cases were no-crimed. In three cases suspects were not identified, three were NFA-ed and one case was discontinued by the CPS.

---

9   Percentages do not always sum to 100 due to rounding or missing information.
10 A suspect was cautioned in four cases – two involving rape and two involving unlawful sexual intercourse (USI) involving very young suspects.

Almost all were acquaintance attacks occurring indoors, with some consensual contact prior to the attack and little evidence of violence. Evidential difficulties are inherent in group attacks: a complainant might find it difficult to remember the sequence of events, including who allegedly raped her and in what order. This makes the job of preparing a watertight case difficult and the police will be all too aware that, if the case does get to court, the defence will exploit any inconsistencies.

In ten cases, one suspect raped two or more complainants. Just two of these cases dropped out as NFA's.

Recent complaint and the complainant's demeanour[11]

No association was found between the speed with which an attack was reported and whether it was no-crimed, although lawyers and barristers thought quick reporting strengthened a complainant's story. However, police interviews also revealed a general feeling that a greater number of 'historical' rapes than ever before are now being reported, with an increased social awareness and acceptance of abuse, especially of children. This has been fostered by the work of organisations like Childline.

In some cases it was felt that a woman's demeanour was important. It is commonly expected that, in the aftermath of a rape, a victim's trauma will be reflected in their being hysterical and tearful.

> "... it's something that has to be covered in the statement really, why, you know they haven't reported it to you for two weeks or something, or seemed calm when they did. It could be that there's a genuine reason you know, but it doesn't look good on paper, does it?"

Therefore, it seems that a complainant's demeanour following an alleged rape was thought to be important, when it should not be. Various research studies confirm the existence of 'Rape Trauma Syndrome' – many victims exhibit a controlled response and in fact mask their feelings, appearing calm and composed (Holmstrom and Burgess, 1978). It is clearly important that police and prosecutors should not read too much into the complainant's demeanour.

Age of complainant

Table 3.4 shows how the attrition process operated for different age groups.

---

11   A report on child abuse cases by Gwyn Davis also discusses aspects such as recent complaint and the complainant's demeanour when giving evidence.

Table 3.4: **Age of complainant and case outcome (pre-court)**

	12 & under %	13-15 %	16-25 %	26-35 %	Over 35 %	All %
No further action	27	28	51	75	69	49
Caution	3	3	1	-	-	1
Charged	67	50	29	15	20	50
TOTAL (n)	100 (29)	100 (88)	100 (165)	100 (94)	100 (68)	100 (305)

Note: n=298 of 305 crimed and detected rapes for which complainant's age and case outcome were known).

Cases where the complainant was under 16 at the time of the alleged attack were most likely to proceed to court. Cases with complainants under 16 had the lowest NFA rate and ultimately the highest conviction rate. One factor is that, even if lack of consent cannot be proved, intercourse with a girl under 16 is illegal; so a USI (unlawful sexual intercourse) charge might be substituted, as happened with three cases in this study.

Violence and injury

Violence was recorded in around 60 per cent of crimed cases. Mostly this amounted to rough treatment such as pushing but sometimes involved beating, punching and kicking. Perhaps unsurprisingly, cases involving strangers were the most likely to be violent, as well as those involving complainants between 16 and 25. Three-quarters of stranger attacks involved violence. In 11 of these incidents the attacker threatened the complainant with a weapon, usually a knife, and in four other cases he threatened to kill her.

Of the 211 women for whom some level of violence was recorded, four suffered fractured or broken bones or cuts requiring stitches. Two of these women, plus a further two, were hospitalised. Of the remainder:

- nearly 100 received physical injury (other than the alleged rape) including mild bruising, scratches or bite marks;

- 34 suffered vaginal or anal cuts or hymenal tears;

- 31 suffered more severe bruising, including black eyes and lacerations.

Consent

In more than half the cases in this study where information about defence deployed by the suspect was available, the main defence relied upon was one of consent. Consent was relied upon in 62 per cent of cases involving acquaintances and half of those involving intimates. In one-quarter of cases, the suspect totally denied the offence. These cases usually involved stranger attacks or intimates.

CPS advice

The police sought CPS advice on whether to charge in 63 cases – 20 per cent of cases in which there was a detected suspect. Where the police sought advice, the CPS recommended no further action in two-thirds of cases. They asked for additional information in ten cases, all of which involved younger complainants.[12] The rate at which the CPS recommended no further action – at 66 per cent – may seem high. However, the police seek advice mainly where the evidence is problematic and the CPS may simply confirm that the prospects of success are low. From interviews, it was clear that advice was often sought in cases where the police, for their part, felt that it would probably be right to drop the case.

Interviews with CPS lawyers indicated that they would like to see more requests for advice in rape cases than at present, and this might result in fewer discontinuances. This is not always possible before the police must charge or release the suspect, but they can (and often do) bail the suspect to return to the police station, and this provides time to consult.

Further issues arising from interviews

Complainant withdrawals

Where the complainant does not wish to give evidence the case could not normally proceed. With intimates, withdrawal sometimes happens because the complainant is reunited with the suspect. Emotional and financial dependence was felt by police and lawyers to be a common reason for a woman feeling unable to pursue the allegation. In one case a complainant's statement revealed that she wished to withdraw her allegation, although she still maintained that she had been raped: if her husband went to prison and lost his job, she would lose everything.

---

12   In these cases, eight suspects were subsequently charged and while proceedings against four were later discontinued by the CPS, two were convicted – one for rape.

In interviews with police officers, it was suggested that it was important for them to warn the complainant about possible evidential difficulties with her case and what would happen if she went to court. The following quotes make the same basic point, but with different emphasis.

> *"You have to sort of look after them and at the same time explain the process so that you reassure them that what they are doing is the best possible course of action in order that we can investigate it properly."*

> *"We would always explain to them that they are going to get a hard time, we don't sort of paint a rosy picture especially if... it's one of consent but we'll say that we will support them as much as we can and we are behind them. And we sort of prepare them for what they are going to face and a lot of them realise that."*

> *"... if you do really think that it is going to be very difficult to prove, is it worth putting the victim through that and going to court and for them to find a jury don't convict the person and then sometimes they could end up well nobody's believed me at the end of the day, which is another sort of trauma for her."*

In warning complainants about the difficulty of securing a conviction, the police might put complainants off pursuing their case without meaning to. The four complainants who were interviewed felt that the police had actively encouraged them to withdraw their allegations. One complainant was told in no uncertain terms that the evidence in her case was weak, even given her injuries:

> *"I showed them my bruises right... and do you know what they said, 'your bruises are not good enough'. I went 'well what do you mean my bruises are not good enough, I've just been raped for God's sake, you don't talk to me like that' - 'your bruises ain't good enough, you've got no case.'"*

The manner in which the police deal with a complainant will obviously affect the way she feels. Even if they do not tell her to withdraw her allegation in so many words, she might be left feeling that it is her only option. An extreme example of this involved one complainant who recalled being taken to the police station where two male CID officers sat with her in a room and questioned her. She said that suggestions were made to her that sometimes women allege rape when it is not in fact true, and that her experience was likely to have been consensual given that the suspect was an ex-boyfriend of hers. Further, she alleged that, as far as they were concerned, blood which was found at the scene of the incident was seen as indicative only of 'rough sex' having occurred. At no point did the officers apparently take a statement from her, apart from recording her eventual decision to withdraw.

"They didn't actually let me speak, I never wrote a statement with them, only to retract my complaint, that's all I did. And that wasn't my idea."

Police and CPS lawyers cited other factors which might encourage rape complainants to withdraw their allegations. They thought that certain ethnic communities and religious groups put pressure on complainants to withdraw their allegations. Orthodox Jews were mentioned as one example. It was suggested that there needs to be more specific police training, so that they are better equipped to deal with sensitivities of this sort. As one lawyer put it:

"It may be difficult in [a big city] to cope with the diversity sometimes... police are not always experienced enough or trained enough to deal with pressures from cultural groups."

Each of the complainants spoken to maintained that if they were raped again they would not report the attack to the police. Of course, too few complainants were interviewed to be able to generalise from their experiences. However, other research supports these findings. A study by Jennifer Temkin (1999), for example, documents the negative perception of rape victims about the way their cases were dealt with. Most complaints were of the disbelieving attitudes of the police and the insensitive ways in which cases were handled.

It should be pointed out that some stations attach a high priority to the care and support given to rape victims. This is reflected in initiatives such as the introduction of victim suites, often away from police premises, the appointment of chaperones in some forces, improved channels of communication to keep victims updated, improved training for officers of both genders and specialist help provided through Victim Support. However, until such initiatives become the rule as opposed to the exception and involve all those concerned, the task of improving police services is not yet complete (Adler, 1991; Temkin, 1999; Victim Support, 1996).

Communication

Good communication is vital if cases are to be pursued effectively.

"The main problem for a woman after the initial investigation was undoubtedly the general lack of information resulting in feelings of helplessness and non-involvement."

Chambers and Millar (1986)

Temkin (1999) reports that, often, the complainant, having given her statement, never hears from the police again. Although the present study was not able to explore this issue systematically, two of the complainants who were interviewed in this study were critical.

> *"... I had no idea what was going on with the police, what they were doing about it, and really if it was all over, you know... like I had been sent home with a smacked bottom. But they were in touch with [the suspect], telling him what was going on and what was going to happen."*

There is a clear need for communication, liaison and skills with dealing with diverse communities. This relates to all those who come into contact with rape complainants, from the police and medical examiners to bodies like Rape Crisis and Victim Support, to name two that already exist and serve to facilitate this.

Vulnerable adults

Forty cases in which the police decided not to bring charges involved complainants who had learning disabilities or were mentally disordered[13]. Sometimes it was thought that the complainant would not make a convincing witness. In addition, allegations of rape by complainants suffering from mental disorder were sometimes considered to be a 'cry for help' or 'attention-seeking'. Often, these women had made similar allegations in the past. Despite the police sometimes believing that the complainant had probably been raped, they were concerned that the stress of a trial might damage her health.

'Second-guessing' the CPS and the jury

One effect of the decrease in no-criming has been that the NFA filter is catching more cases. A major change since the previous study is that the CPS, rather than the police, now makes the decision whether or not to proceed with a prosecution, which obviously changes the dynamics of the whole prosecution process. The police are likely to draw on their experience of what the CPS will support, just as the CPS, in reviewing the evidence, will have regard to how a jury will view it. As one police officer put it:

> *"... we tend to work backwards from experience... because when you have had your fingers burned in Crown Court a few times and asked a question why didn't you do this, or why did you do that, and you think, oh God I hadn't thought of that, those experiences burn on your mind as the same for all of us, so when you come to deal with a case later we tend to look at where we are going with it, and work back to provide all the issues that will help us to get there."*

---

13   Twenty-two cases involving women suffering from mental disorder or learning disabilities were no-crimed, usually because their allegations were believed to be false, and 18 were NFA-ed.

However, an alternative perspective is that the police should not act as 'gatekeepers' and should, to a large extent, investigate a case and submit it for prosecution regardless of the way in which it is likely to be perceived by the CPS.

> *"Whatever the CPS think ultimately, it's still our duty to investigate it as thoroughly as possible, and although perhaps in the back of your mind you might think... really we haven't got any corroboration all we're going to have is his word against hers... it's still our duty to investigate."*

For its part, in reviewing the case the CPS must decide whether the evidence is likely to persuade a jury. For example, is there corroboration by way of medical or forensic evidence? Are there independent witnesses? Is there evidence of violence? As one CPS lawyer said:

> *"We might believe that [a complainant] will come up to proof but convincing a jury is a different thing... at the end of the day the jury in a 95 per cent date rape case will say 'sorry, we are not going to send this guy to jail for seven years because the woman, you know, met him and went with him quite willingly.'"*

This may point to a need for better training and evidence-gathering for the police, including collection and presentation of expert evidence. There is a particular need to ensure that full use is made of any evidence of injury.

4. CPS decision-making

If the police decide to charge a suspect, the case is passed to the CPS for a decision on whether to proceed with a prosecution. The CPS must decide whether prosecution is appropriate applying the evidential and public interest tests set out in the Code for Crown Prosecutors. Firstly, is there enough evidence to provide a 'realistic prospect of conviction': would a jury, properly directed, be more likely than not to convict the defendant? If there is insufficient evidence, the case cannot proceed. Secondly, if there is sufficient evidence, is it in the public interest to proceed? It is highly unlikely that it would not be in the public interest to prosecute a rape case because rape is a serious offence, likely to result in a significant sentence, where the victim is likely to be vulnerable, put in considerable fear and attacked – all factors in favour of prosecution set out in the Code. Figure 4.1 shows what happened to those cases submitted to the CPS.

Half the cases crimed and detected by the police were submitted to the CPS for prosecution. The CPS discontinued just over one-quarter of these cases[14]. About half these were discontinued at or before the first court hearing, 16 per cent before the second hearing and the remainder at or after the second court hearing.

In discussion, the CPS maintained that they always try to press ahead with prosecution and would not discontinue without very good reason. There was only limited information as to the nature of evidential weaknesses, although in five cases the witness's refusal to give evidence was noted on file.

---

14   This compares with the national discontinuance rate of 12 per cent for 1996.

Figure 4.1: Flow diagram illustrating the attrition of rape cases from charge to conviction (percentages)
(base = defendants charged; n=140)[15]

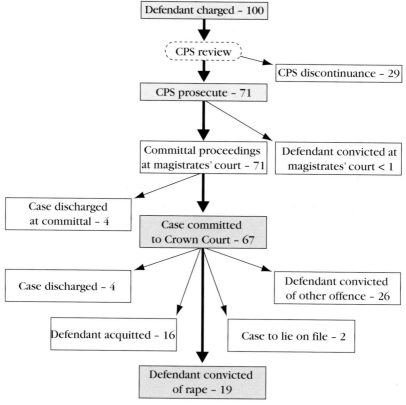

Sexual assault cases in general and rape cases in particular raise a number of evidential difficulties:

● they often involve vulnerable victims, including children and those with mental health problems or learning disabilities;

● the victim's sexual history is sometimes an issue;

● there is often a prior relationship between victim and offender which can test the victim's willingness to give evidence – and the victim can pull out at any point in the process, effectively leaving the prosecution without a case;

● with most other crimes it is clear that a criminal act has occurred; with sex offences involving those over 16 the issue commonly turns on the issue of consent – simply his word against hers.

---

15 Percentages do not always sum to 100 due to rounding or missing information.

There were mixed views about how far the system should have regard to the welfare of the complainant. Some police officers and CPS lawyers felt that a rape case should be given a chance in court in borderline cases. However, one CPS lawyer argued that it was right for the decision on prosecution to be distanced from the complainant.

"I know that a lot of people think that... you should give the victim her day in court, but I don't think that is right at all... I think the victim doesn't really have much of a say whether you discontinue the case or not, it has to be just between the officer and yourself."

The research examined the link between CPS decision-making and features of the case. There was found to be a significant association between the age of the complainant and whether a case was discontinued. Cases involving particularly young complainants (under 12 years old) or older complainants (over 45 years old) were those most likely to be proceeded with by the CPS. (see Table 4.1).

Table 4.1:   Age of complainant and CPS action

	12 & under %	13–15 %	16–25 %	26–35 %	36–45 %	Over 45 %	All %
Discontinued	14	34	33	29	17	-	28
Prosecuted	86	66	67	71	83	100	72
TOTAL (n)	100 (21)	100 (44)	100 (49)	100 (14)	100 (6)	100 (7)	100 (147)

Note: n=141 of 147 rapes where a suspect was charged for which age of complainant was known.

No significant association was found between other case circumstances, such as consensual contact, and the CPS decision to discontinue cases.

Two alleged acquaintance rape cases and four involving intimates were recorded as having been dropped on public interest grounds[16]. However, closer examination suggested that these cases involved complainants who were reluctant to give evidence and so could more accurately have been recorded as discontinued on evidential grounds[17].

---

16   These included husband and wife or boyfriend and girlfriend cases and ones involving young children.
17   It was sometimes difficult to distinguish between a public interest discontinuance and a complainant withdrawal as the same event was often recorded in different ways as cases proceeded through the CPS stage.

5. The progress of rape cases through the courts

Magistrates' courts and the Crown Court

Rape is an indictable-only offence and therefore must be tried at the Crown Court. All cases start off in the magistrates' court[18] but can only be finalised there if they are reduced to lesser offences such as indecent assault or unlawful sexual intercourse (USI)[19] or are discontinued prior to or at committal. Court proceedings were brought against 100 defendants. Of the initial sample of crimed cases, only 26 per cent reached the Crown Court. One defendant was convicted and sentenced at the magistrates' court for USI.

When cases were first heard at a magistrates' court 88 defendants were charged with rape and five with attempted rape. A further three defendants were charged with USI and another two with indecent assault[20]. Sixty-six defendants faced additional or alternative charges, 43 of which were sexual offences.

Figure 5.1 gives an overview of what happened to the 100 defendants who were prosecuted.

---

18   Indictable-only offences will be sent straight to the Crown Court under the Crime and Disorder Act 1998.
19   Such cases are triable either at magistrates' court or Crown Court.
20   Two defendants were charged with non-sexual offences including false imprisonment.

Figure 5.1: Flow diagram illustrating the attrition of rape cases from prosecution to conviction (percentages)
(Base = prosecuted cases; n=100)

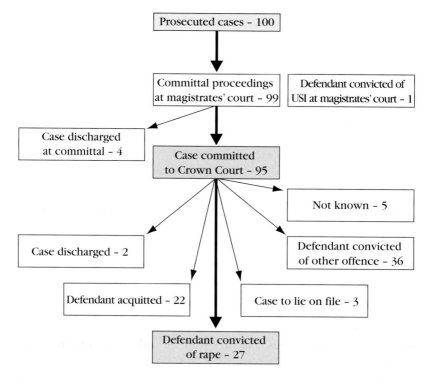

Case outcomes

Table 5.1 shows convictions for both rape and alternative charges, and details of acquittals, according to type of rape.

Table 5.1: **Outcome at the Crown Court**

	Stranger (n)	Acquaintance (n)	Intimate (n)	All (n)
Convicted of rape	2	13	10	25
Convicted of attempted rape	1	1	-	2
Convicted: USI under 16	-	5	5	10
Convicted: USI under 13	-	1	1	2
Convicted: indecent assault	2	8	7	17
Convicted: incest	-	-	2	2
Convicted: other non-sexual offence	1	-	4	5
Jury acquittal	2	8	6	16
Judge ordered acquittal	-	1	1	2
Judge directed acquittal	-	1	3	4
Other	-	2	3	5
Not known	-	3	2	5
TOTAL (n)	8	43	44	95

Note: n=95 (Crown Court defendant sample)

In all, 63 offenders were convicted of an offence at the Crown Court. Of these, 25 were convicted of rape and two of attempted rape. Only 9 per cent of the original sample of 299 suspects for crimed rapes were convicted of rape or attempted rape. This compares with the national conviction rate of 10 per cent at the time of the research in 1996. Among the remaining 36, 17 were convicted of indecent assault and 12 for USI.

Table 5.1 shows that a number of defendants in cases involving acquaintances or intimates were convicted of USI but (as one would expect) no stranger defendants were. A significant minority of defendants in all three relationship groups were convicted of indecent assault. These were not necessarily less serious offences: indecent assault carries a maximum sentence of ten years. One stranger was convicted of assault occasioning grievous bodily harm. Four intimates were convicted of other non-sexual offences which included assault or affray: this might indicate that these incidents were associated with domestic violence.

Plea

Figure 5.2: Defendant pleas at the Crown Court

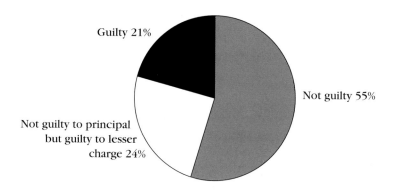

Figure 5.2 shows defendant pleas at the Crown Court.

Three-quarters of those defendants who pleaded guilty to a lesser charge were convicted only of those charges. (In the remaining cases the plea was not accepted and the case went to trial.) Interviews with judges and barristers confirmed that plea-bargaining, or 'horse trading' as one judge called it, often takes place. Relative certainty of conviction and sparing the complainant from having to give evidence can be persuasive factors when considering whether to hold out for a rape conviction.

Defendants in both alleged acquaintance and intimate rapes were more likely than strangers to plead guilty to an alternative offence. Intimate cases often involve children and it may be difficult to establish whether all the legal components of a rape charge have been made out. In these circumstances, a charge of indecent assault is often substituted.

Age

Cases involving particularly young complainants (especially under 13 years of age) were more likely to result in conviction:

- 88 per cent of cases reaching the Crown Court involving complainants under the age of 13 led to a conviction;

- three-quarters of cases involving complainants aged 16 to 25 led to a conviction;

- Only half those cases involving women over 25 reaching the Crown Court resulted in a conviction.

Acquittals

One-quarter of all cases reaching Crown Court resulted in an acquittal, usually by a jury. There was no significant variation in the acquittal rate between the three relationship groups or between age groups, although cases involving older complainants (over 26) were more likely to lead to acquittal at court than those involving younger complainants. However, a few cases where the complainant and suspect were known to one another resulted in:

- judge directed acquittals – where, after hearing the prosecution evidence, the judge decided that the prosecution had not presented sufficient evidence to prove its case (four cases);

- judge ordered acquittals - where the prosecution offered no evidence at the outset of the trial because the key witness did not appear (two cases).

Sentences

Table 5.2 shows the sentences given to those convicted of rape or other offences.

Table 5.2: **Sentence by offence type**

	Rape (n)	Attempted rape (n)	Other offences (n)
Up to 12 months	1	-	8
1-2 years	1	-	7
>2-4 years	4	1	7
>4-6 years	7	1	3
>6 years	9	-	4
Life	3	-	-
Community service	-	-	1
Probation			3
Supervision order			1
Conditional discharge	-	-	2
TOTAL	25	2	36

Note: n=63 (those defendants who were convicted at Crown Court).

All those convicted of rape or attempted rape were imprisoned, in most cases for more than four years and in three cases for life. Among the 36 defendants convicted of offences other than rape, 29 were imprisoned, and the remaining seven received community sentences or conditional discharges.

The figure below gives an indication of national sentencing figures for rape and attempted rape at the time of the research. It indicates that where a defendant is convicted of rape, the sentence is likely to be severe:

- half those convicted of rape incurred custodial sentences of over six years up to life; and

- just under 30 per cent incurred sentences of between four and six years.

Figure 5.3: Proportion of males sentenced[21] to immediate custody for offences of rape and attempted rape of a female, England and Wales 1996

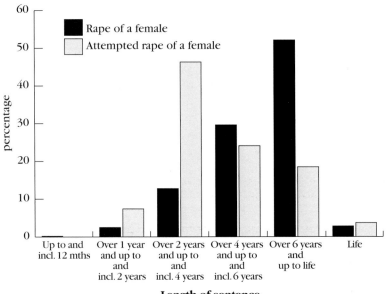

21   Total males sentenced at the Crown Court for the offence of rape of a female was 478 of which 465 were given a custodial sentence, 29 detained under s53 of the Children and Young Persons Act 1933, 3 Restriction Order, 3 Probation Order, 2 Hospital Order, 2 fully suspended sentence, 1 absolute discharge, 1 Supervision Order and 1 otherwise dealt with. Total males sentenced at the Crown Court for the offence of attempted rape of a female was 63 of which 54 were given a custodial sentence, 5 detained under s53 of the Children and Young Persons Act 1933, 2 Hospital Order, 1 Probation Order and 1 Supervision Order.

6. Practitioners' views of the court process

Because the number of cases reaching court covered by this study was quite small, interviews with CPS lawyers, barristers and judges were important in exploring some of the issues underlying the statistical findings.

The number and nature of rape cases reaching court

The number of cases reaching the Crown Court increased from 758 in 1985 to 1,341 in 1997. Judges and barristers confirmed that the *types* of rape case reaching court had changed over the last ten years or so. But interviewees suggested that this was because the filtering of cases by the police and CPS was *less* rigorous than in the past, notwithstanding the fact that the proportion of initially recorded rapes reaching court has fallen.

> *"... you used to only get the strong cases going to court, whereas now... you've got far more weak rapes going to court than any other category of case."* [Barrister]

In fact, as Appendix A shows, the proportion of rape cases that reach court has declined markedly over the years. But the study shows that the *nature* of cases proceeding to court has changed (i.e. more acquaintance/intimate rapes), reflecting changes in the nature of cases reported. The case now usually turns on the issue of consent, which puts into context the perceptions that cases are 'weaker' than they used to be.

> *"What is happening now... is that a very much larger proportion of cases of rape now depend on one person's word against another's."* [Barrister]

The notion that there are 'types' of rape permeates the court process, as exemplified by the following comment from a judge.

> *"... I wonder whether the serious type of rape of a stranger... in a public place or whatever at night should not be a rather separate offence than, if I can put it to the other end of the scale, the misunderstanding between two people who know each other."*

Other respondents suggested that in cases where the complainant and suspect are known to each other, there are also more likely to be false allegations.

> *"The weaker cases, the simply word against word cases, you are going to get a higher percentage of cases in which there is a fraudulent allegation, you are bound to, I think it's inevitable."*
> [Barrister]

This barrister went so far as to suggest that perhaps it is more likely that false allegations of rape reach court, the genuine complainant having withdrawn her complaint because she cannot face the ordeal of a trial. However, there was no evidence that this view was widely shared.

The trial

Once it is decided that a case will go to court, the CPS instructs a barrister to represent it at the trial. Barristers interviewed felt that the standard of cases presented to them by the CPS was generally good and that papers were received in good time. But sometimes a case conference involving the CPS, police and barrister could be a helpful means of ensuring that any weaknesses could be addressed in good time. For example, if there is reference to violence, is there supporting photographic or medical evidence?

Where the issue is one of consent, the defence has little choice but to seek to undermine the credibility of the complainant. To this end, it may seek to exploit details of her sexual history or mental health.

Experienced judges can be given a 'sex ticket' which authorises them to preside over serious sex cases such as rape, and training is given. There was a widespread view that barristers ideally should have had several years experience before tackling rape trials, which call for a degree of specialism. However, one barrister criticised the CPS for the level of fees they attach to rape cases. In general, the more serious the case the higher the fee and, therefore, the more senior the barrister who will take the case. It was suggested that the CPS send rape cases to chambers with relatively small fees attached, which would preclude senior barristers from taking them.

> *"It's not that the good people and experienced people are holding out for silly money... I mean we'll accept the fact that we'll get paid half what the defence barrister is going to get but just don't pay us a quarter of what the other guy is going to get, that's simply insulting and we won't do it."*

The view echoes *The Review of the Crown Prosecution Service* (the Glidewell report) which recommended that fees paid to prosecution counsel should be in line with those paid to the defence[22].

The jury

"It's a matter for the jury. It is not a matter for a police officer, a lawyer, a judge or anyone else."

With most rapes involving people known to the victim, the task usually facing the jury is to decide whether or not the complainant consented and, if she did not, whether the defendant was reckless as to consent. The requirement that the jury must be satisfied 'beyond reasonable doubt' in cases which hinge on her word against his sets a tough challenge for the prosecution. Nevertheless, judges and barristers interviewed did not believe that juries have too much problem with rape trials. There was a view that the prosecution prefers to see a jury made up predominantly of men, as it was thought that women tend to be judgmental of their own sex and might have less sympathy for the complainant. One police interview offered a rather different perspective.

"It is a judgement call, these people are sitting in their jury room and they think that some of them are blokes and they have gone out at a night on the town and they have had a few beers and they chatted up a girl and then they have made a pass at her and got a brush off, but thought oh my goodness, what would I have done if... and that is the area where people think do I really put this nice bloke from the students union into prison for this for rape when, you know, they were both drunk as skunks, etc., etc."

Sentencing

Judges interviewed stated that evidence of violence was always an important factor in sentencing. Other aggravating factors included: indulgence in perversion; infliction of more than one sexual act on the complainant; and the use of a weapon. In addition, an incident involving a breach of trust, perhaps where the complainant was in the care of the defendant, might result in a more punitive sentence.

---

22   Recent analysis has shown that, on average, CPS fees are about 66 per cent of the value of fees paid to defence counsel out of the Graduated Fee Scheme. The gap may be larger for rape cases for which the defence are often able to obtain a Legal Aid Certificate for leading counsel

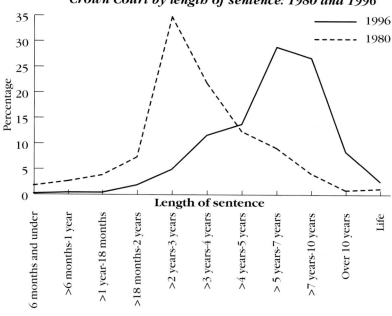

Figure 6.1: *Males sentenced to imprisonment for rape at the Crown Court by length of sentence: 1980 and 1996*

Source: Criminal statistics.

As a result of *Billam*[23], and perhaps pressure from the public and women's groups, sentences for rape offences have increased over the years (see Figure 6.1). Some of the judges interviewed believed that, as a result of stiffer sentences, juries are now less likely to convict.

> *"A five-year starting point for a contested trial is too high... if it's a date rape thing, and [the jury] think 'possibly it was rape, but it's not worth five years.'"*

Judges were not unanimous, however: another believed that sentences are still too low, especially for 'date rape' cases. The relevance of plea was summed up by one judge.

> *"I think we all regard a plea of guilty in a sex case as deserving an even greater discount than it does in any other case because of not putting the girl through the ordeal."*

---

23   The then Lord Chief Justice, Lord Lane, in his summary to the *R v Billam* case (February 1986) set out the following
     sentencing guidelines:
   i.   rape committed by an adult without any aggravating or mitigating factors in a contested case (i.e. not guilty
        plea) - five years starting point;
   ii. rape committed by two or more men acting together, or by a man who has broken into or otherwise gained
        access, or by a person in a position of responsibility, or who abducts the victim - eight years starting point;
   iii. defendants who have committed a campaign of rape on a number of different women - 15 years or more;
   iv. where the defendant has perverted or psychopathic tendencies or gross personality disorder and where he is
        likely to remain a danger for some time - life sentence is not inappropriate.

Indeed, several judges suggested that the *Billam* guidelines are not as helpful as they were because the nature of the cases now coming before the courts is different.

> *"I believe that I have presided over a number of what we will call date rape cases in which, given my own total discretion, I would not have given him five years."*

Who makes a good witness?

> *"Someone who is telling the truth – it's as simple as that."* [Barrister]

There appeared to be a wide range of views as to what made a complainant convincing when she was standing in the witness box. From the prosecution point of view, a witness who breaks down sobbing in the witness box was said to be 'cosmetically effective' in some cases. On the other hand, a well-prepared complainant was also seen as a strong witness. From the defence point of view, it would usually be counter-productive to cause a complainant avoidable distress. It was felt that particularly young or particularly old complainants often make good witnesses, as a jury will tend to judge them as unlikely to lie.

> *"If you've got a child under ten and... she says you know, this man put his penis in my vagina, you think well it's more likely they are telling the truth because a child under ten wouldn't know that grown-ups do that sort of thing."*

Teenage witnesses were felt to be more problematic. According to one barrister, teenage girls have been known to make allegations as a way of attention-seeking. It was also alleged that sometimes young girls indulging in sexual activities might claim that it was without consent when they were confronted by a parent.

Perhaps surprisingly, prostitutes were said to be convincing witnesses. It was felt that, given the nature of a prostitute's work, they are unlikely to 'cry rape'. In addition, rapes of prostitutes are often violent and evidence of injury will usually count in support of an allegation. As one police officer said:

> *"I regard them as business people. Why would they want to take God knows how many hours out of their tour of duty when they could be making money to make up a spurious story?... and most prostitutes you know they're pretty strong people and unless there is an overt weapon that can do them harm, they're not going to let somebody get the better of them... so you usually find some supportive evidence of violence."*

Consistency of evidence was seen as particularly important. This is not always easy as an account is likely to have been provided several times: to the first person the complainant tells after the attack; to the police; in response to questions from the medical examiner; and in her cross-examination at court. The defence will draw attention to any discrepancies in a woman's story.

Some cases may appear weak on the surface but, when given a chance in court, result in a conviction. One judge spoke about a case in which a complainant had returned home with a group of men intending to have intercourse with one of them but on the way deciding that she would rather have intercourse with another. However, when the second man had later tried to have intercourse with her she pushed him off and ran out of the flat. The incident was recorded as rape and, as the judge said, there was very little evidence to support the allegation and a conviction appeared highly unlikely. However, the case was proceeded with, the complainant turned out to be a good witness and when it went before a jury they found the defendant guilty.

The use of sexual history evidence

The Sexual Offences (Amendment) Act 1976 sought to protect a complainant of rape from the unrestricted admission at trial of evidence relating to, or cross-examination about, her previous sexual experiences with people other than the accused. It is now for the judge to decide whether sexual history evidence should be admitted. In addition to this, measures are being introduced in the Youth Justice and Criminal Evidence Bill which give further restrictions upon what evidence of an alleged victim's sexual behaviour can be considered relevant.

Judges and barristers were generally of the opinion that the sexual history of a complainant was often relevant to a case. They felt that blocking such evidence might present a false picture to the jury.

> "If you were sitting on the jury and that was the issue - in the back of the car, did she consent or did she not - would you not want to know whether she has slept with the last five men that she went to the dance hall with?" [Judge]

Another judge took the opposite view.

> "Normally, whether a girl has consented with this man has got nothing to do with whether she has consented with another. It is wrong simply to say to a girl 'you will go with anybody', because she may go with anybody except him."

Some respondents thought sexual history might be relevant, but only if it showed that the complainant was lying: for example, if she claimed that she was a virgin at the time of the alleged attack and the defence can show her to have slept with someone in the past. Evidence that she has lied about some part of the allegation has implications for her other evidence. It can also remove the element of aggravation that the victim was a virgin.

The complainant's sexual history was not raised in the handful of cases observed, and information about admission of sexual history evidence was not available from the files examined for the statistical exercise.

Easing the trauma for the complainant

When a complainant is called to give her evidence in court, the prosecution may ask the judge for a screen to be erected so that the complainant cannot see the defendant. One-way glass from the public gallery, whereby the public can watch proceedings but cannot be seen or heard from the court, was mentioned by barristers and judges as another way to make the complainant feel at ease. It has been suggested that having a complainant give evidence via a video link from a separate room (particularly in the case of vulnerable witnesses) might go some way further towards easing her trauma (Home Office report: 'Speaking Up For Justice', 1998[24]). However, CPS lawyers, judges and barristers did not see this as a good idea in the general run of cases. It was felt that a complainant can have a more positive impact on the jury by giving evidence in person, as implied by one judge.

"In some cases I think that the jury do regard the whole thing as just another television programme... if you can possibly put... flesh and blood on the witness stand you are going to find a much more convincing prosecution case than if you don't."

There is no evidence from child abuse cases that having evidence presented via a video link makes any difference to the outcome of a case. So this difficulty may be more imagined than real. The answer is probably that different approaches are needed in different circumstances. There is a need to balance the possible (but unproven) risk that the jury will be less directly affected by the victim if she gives the evidence through a live link with the risk that without the protection of a live link some victims will either not pursue their case through to court, or will be very distressed by the process of giving evidence. The Interdepartmental Working Group on the treatment of Vulnerable or Intimidated Witnesses in the Criminal Justice System made recommendations which focus on the needs of the witnesses, rather than on the offence. Recommendations in its report propose the development of

---

24   Report of the Interdepartmental Working Group on the Treatment of Vulnerable or Intimidated Witnesses in the Criminal Justice System.

training materials which will enable all practitioners in the criminal justice system to have at least a minimal level of awareness of vulnerable or intimidated witness issues. Rape is one of a number of offences which can involve especially vulnerable victims, by virtue of age, mental illness or learning disabilities.

Delays in cases coming to court were considered to be another source of anxiety and strain for the complainant. This can be very frustrating for the prosecution if not for the defence. As one barrister put it:

"The defence and the defendant have a vested interest in delay."

Delays and adjournments can occur when the court is waiting for forensic evidence. However, this would usually only be where a case rests on the identification of a suspect and such cases are relatively unusual. Generally, respondents felt that rape cases are not necessarily more subject to delays than any other kind of case, and that the difficulties are part of the more general problem of delay. The provisions in the Crime and Disorder Act 1998 for indictable-only cases such as rape to start in the Crown Court should help reduce court delays, once rolled out nationally[25].

---

25   The indictable-only provisions are currently being piloted in six areas of England and Wales.

7. Discussion

This study has examined the processing of rape cases by the criminal justice system and pointed to the stages at which cases fall by the wayside. Figure 7.1 provides an overview of the process and shows that of every 100 cases in the study, only six resulted in a conviction for rape.

Figure 7.1: The overall attrition process for cases in the study (actual proportions) N=483[26]

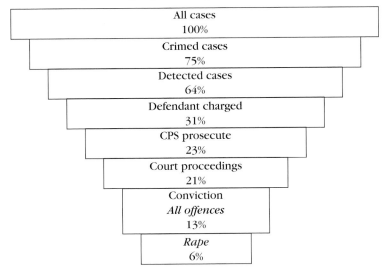

All cases
100%
Crimed cases
75%
Detected cases
64%
Defendant charged
31%
CPS prosecute
23%
Court proceedings
21%
Conviction
All offences
13%
Rape
6%

The national statistics of rape offences show a similar picture.

The proportion of recorded rapes resulting in a defendant being convicted for rape was lower in 1997, at nine per cent, than in any other year except 1994. However, since 1985, the number of recorded rapes has increased more than three-fold.

The problem of attrition in the criminal justice system, and its increase over time, is not restricted to rape offences. A recent study (Langan and Farrington, 1998) examined changes in attrition between 1981 and 1995 for a variety of offences ranging from murder and rape to motor vehicle theft.

---

26   483 cases is the sample on which complete information is available – from recording to conviction.

The study showed that the risk of being caught and convicted had fallen for all the offences considered. While the proportions of alleged rapists convicted fell by 63 per cent there was a similar fall for assault (66%). The increase for rape partly reflects changes in reporting, which itself may reflect greater confidence that the police will deal sympathetically with complainants. But it also means that most of the increase centres on cases involving acquaintances and intimates, and it has always been these cases that are most likely to be dropped. Nevertheless, the fact that fewer stranger rapes are ending in conviction – mainly because of poorer detection rates – is a cause for concern.

A point which runs through much of the process is the need for practitioners to have a better understanding of the particular needs of victims of sexual offences. There is also a link with some of the concerns about other offences, notably those involving domestic violence, in that the prior relationship between victim and offender can make the practical and emotional issues particularly difficult to handle. It is especially difficult for a victim to persevere with a case of length when she may be in a continuing relationship with the accused, or if pressure may be brought to bear through other social contacts or networks.

Despite the explanations, it is cause for concern that only 6 per cent of those initially accused of rape were convicted of rape or attempted rape. The figure rises to 9 per cent if no-crimed cases are removed and to 21 per cent if convictions for any offence are included, but these are still low. The problem is not primarily that cases are not cleared up – in the great majority of cases the identity of the alleged offender is known. But it is precisely because the victim so often knows the offender that difficulties often arise in pursuing cases to a successful conclusion. This chapter looks at the key points at which cases drop out of the system, and what more might be done to secure convictions.

No-criming

One quarter of incidents initially recorded as rape are subsequently no-crimed by the police.

Cases should only be no-crimed where there is clear evidence that the allegation was fabricated. The research suggests that, although fewer cases are no-crimed than used to be, many are wrongly no-crimed rather than being NFA-ed. For example, it was found that in some instances the reason for no-criming was that there was insufficient evidence.

Recommendations

1. The existing guidance on restricting the circumstances in which cases may be no-crimed remains valid. Consideration should be given to its re-issue, and to ensuring that it is adequately covered in police training and in HMIC inspections.

No further action

Half of all cases which are 'crimed' and cleared up result in no further action by the police.

The presumption is that a serious crime has been committed, and in most cases the police know who did it. The most common reason why cases drop out at this stage is that the complainant did not wish to proceed. (This was also a common reason for no-criming, and the reality is that less no-criming would be likely to result in more NFA.) This prompts questions:

- do complainants receive sufficient support to persevere when the case could succeed, or are they too often discouraged by the police?

- do the police set the evidential test too high, perhaps second-guessing the CPS?

- is sufficient use made of evidence of violence?

There are examples of cases succeeding where the initial evidence looked unpromising, and it is almost certain that at least some of the cases which are not proceeded with could result in conviction. But where the case turns on the defendant's evidence against the complainant's, and because a jury must be satisfied 'beyond reasonable doubt' that she is telling the truth and he is lying, it is not surprising that many cases are dropped.

Recommendations

2. Those reporting rape to the police should be given greater support, perhaps involving agencies other than the police. Some other jurisdictions (eg some US states) have involved victims more closely in the investigative process, and have coupled this with support to help them persevere. There are various models which would be worth more thorough investigation.

3. There is a particular problem with intimate and acquaintance rapes, where there is a need to find out in more detail why cases are dropped than was possible in the present study.

4. The police should be readier to consult the CPS in borderline cases, and should not be too quick to assume that cases which may look unpromising could not be built up, especially if the complainant can be drawn more prominently into the process.

5. It is of interest that cases in which there is evidence of violence are often dropped. There would appear to be scope for better evidence gathering, eg through photographs and medical reports, and for ensuring such evidence is given due weight in later discussions.

6. Individual police officers will rarely deal with rape – the number of rapes reported each year is only about one twentieth of the number of police officers. There is a clear need to cover the issues raised by rape cases in training, but also to ensure that refresher training is given as best practice develops.

7. Further research could examine the way in which cases are dealt with and complainants treated at the early stages of the system in order to get a better understanding of why withdrawals occur. This would more clearly identify the dynamics of the process – this was not wholly possible in the present study which was primarily restricted to retrospective analysis of case files.

Discontinuance by the Crown Prosecution Service

Just over one-quarter of cases forwarded to the CPS were discontinued.

The CPS dropped some cases because, despite having persevered through the earlier stages, the complainant decided not to co-operate. Sometimes this happened before the case reached court; in other cases later. On other occasions the CPS reviewed the available evidence and decided that the chances of conviction were not sufficient for there to be a realistic prospect of conviction. This prompts questions about the level of co-operation between the police and CPS where more evidence was needed, and perhaps whether too high a threshold is set.

Anecdotal evidence suggests a need for greater specialisation in the legal profession as there are key features of rape cases which differentiate them from the general norm. Sexual offences are still comparatively rare in terms of court caseloads, and because of non-specialisation, lawyers deal with few sexual cases of any sort, and very rarely with rape.

It is worth citing from the Glidewell report, as it strongly echoes key findings of the present study.

'With some offences... the CPS lawyer has a particularly difficult task in deciding whether to discontinue. A charge of rape, where the defence is consent, is perhaps the most difficult offence on which to make such a judgement on paper. Often, if what the complainant says is believed completely, the defendant was Guilty of rape but, where there are no signs of violence or other facts which tend to support her account, the issue will in the end depend on whether she is believed by a jury. ....This raises the question whether, in some limited circumstances, CPS lawyers should be permitted (as at present they are not) to meet complainants in order to gain a clearer understanding of the alleged circumstances and to decide as best they can whether a complainant is likely to convince a jury.' (Chapter 4 , para 33.)

Recommendations

8. A study, as mentioned above, which tracked cases through in detail with interviews with decision-makers (including complainants) on individual cases, would pick up reasons why the CPS drop cases (and also why they recommend the police not to charge). This would link with a recommendation in the Glidewell report that a study should be made of the reasons for discontinuance in more serious offences.

9. Although in the present study some lawyers expressed reservations about meeting victims, Glidewell offers the idea of meetings with the complainant as an idea worth discussion. The report 'Speaking Up For Justice' makes a recommendation (Recommendation 27) for meetings between the prosecutor and certain vulnerable or intimidated witnesses, claiming that it would assist the presentation of the case and provide reassurance for the witness. It is worth considering the practices of other countries such as the USA, where the equivalent of the CPS does meet with complainants.

Court proceedings

It is not uncommon for charges to be downgraded, typically from rape to indecent assault, when the case comes to trial. There is a difficult balance to be struck between securing a certain conviction to a lesser offence, and downgrading what is a very serious offence. This raises the question of whether the law itself needs any revision. This is a complex issue, since being raped by someone known and trusted can be potentially even more traumatic than being raped by a stranger. So there are no easy answers based on the relationship between complainant and suspect. But given the fact that *only 43 per cent of convictions were for rape or attempted rape*, in effect offences initially recorded as rape are being reclassified as they progress through the criminal justice system. And it would appear that most of this happens late on, given the difference between the offence charged at committal and the outcome at the Crown Court. This is another issue that was picked up in the Glidewell report. It is, however, worth noting that 'lesser' offences sometimes attracted more severe penalties than some rapes; so while rape may have the most severe maximum penalty, there is considerable overlap in the sentences handed out for different offences. This reflects the full range of aggravating and mitigating factors which may be even more important than the precise charge.

There were clear differences of view about when (if ever) the sexual history of the complainant was relevant. The only clear support for such evidence is if it bears on the veracity of the complainant – for example if she claims she was a virgin at the time and there is evidence that she was not. That apart, from interviews with judges, prosecutors and police, the nearest view to a consensus is probably that of the judge who said: *"It is wrong simply to say to a girl 'you will go with anybody', because she may go with anybody except him"*.

The high rate at which complainants withdraw and previous research (Davis and Westcott, 1992) strongly suggest that complainants feel that giving evidence in court would be a harrowing ordeal. Ways of providing better protection in certain types of case were set out in 'Speaking up for Justice', the report of the Interdepartmental Working Group of the Treatment of Vulnerable or Intimidated Witnesses in the Criminal Justice System. As a result, measures are being introduced in the Youth Justice and Criminal Evidence Bill. These cover such issues as physical measures to reduce the stress of giving evidence at trial (such as screens, live link CCTV and pre-recorded interviews); restrictions on the freedom of defendants personally to cross-examine their alleged victims; and further restrictions upon what evidence of an alleged victim's sexual behaviour can be considered relevant.

Glidewell pointed to the imbalance in resources available to the defence and prosecution, with defence fees on average between 50 per cent and 80 per cent higher than those of the prosecution. This echoes points from interviews in the present study.

Recommendations

10. A study of offences with high rates of charge reduction, as recommended in the Glidewell report, would help explain the dynamics behind the change in charges at court.

11. The Review of Sex Offences will provide a useful opportunity to consider whether there should be any changes in the way rape is defined, including whether rape should be 'graded' in some way: the mismatch between initial recording and conviction is clearly unsatisfactory. It runs counter to moves in the wider context of violent offences to settle charges at an early stage, so that these can better inform later decision-making, for example in terms of early guilty pleas.

12. There is a need to improve prosecution standards, and to ensure that prosecuting barristers are paid broadly similarly to defence lawyers to remove possible imbalances between the expertise the two sides bring to the issues.

13. Other points emerging from this research simply reinforce the case for the changes which are already before Parliament, and which are designed to give more protection to vulnerable victims and witnesses.

Further work

There are two particularly important gaps in information which need to be addressed. First, while this study has shown the extent of attrition and the stage at which it occurs, further vital information could be gained from a study which tracked cases through to conclusion, to assess the precise way in which decisions are influenced at each stage.

Second, while it is rarely practicable to import ideas directly from other countries, there are likely to be elements in the way rape cases are dealt with elsewhere that would be worth considering. Some of these have been touched on, but further evidence – for example whether better support for victims has directly helped to reduce attrition – would be worth investigating.

Appendices

Appendix A

Table A.1: *Overall attrition rate for rape between 1985 and 1997*

	Total number of offences recorded by the police as rape		Total number of offences cleared up by the police		Total number of offenders proceeded against at magistrates' court		Total number of offenders committed for trial at Crown Court		Total number of offenders appearing for trial at Crown Court		Total cautioned or found guilty of rape	
	No	%	No	%	No	%	No	%	No	%	No	%
1985	1,842	100	1,177	64	844	46	758	41	569	31	450	24
1986	2,288	100	1,428	62	927	41	804	35	593	26	415	18
1987	2,471	100	1,748	71	1,048	42	867	35	649	26	453	18
1988	2,855	100	2,055	72	1,288	45	1,082	38	799	28	540	19
1989	3,305	100	2,455	74	1,400	42	1,140	34	930	28	613	19
1990	3,391	100	2,498	74	1,467	43	1,147	34	914	27	561	17
1991	4,045	100	3,062	76	1,711	42	1,323	33	914	24	559	14
1992	4,142	100	3,124	75	1,648	40	1,184	29	933	22	529	13
1993	4,589	100	3,403	74	1,704	37	1,202	26	892	19	482	10
1994	5,032	100	3,695	73	1,782	35	1,266	25	940	19	460	9
1995	4,986	100	3,722	75	1,604	32	1,048	21	1,065	21	578	12
1996	5,759	100	4,418	77	1,696	29	1,158	20	1,107	19	573	10
1997	6,281	100	4,946	78	1,880	30	1,341	21	1,209	19	599	9

Notes.
1. Recorded figures and clear-ups (first two columns) do not include no-crimes.
2. Figures in this table are taken from two sources – those in the first two columns are *offence*-based while those in the remaining columns are *offender*-based.

Appendix B

Comparing the two rape studies

The no-criming figure was calculated on a different basis in the previous Home Office study based on 1985 data. The previous study only recorded cases no-crimed at least one-month after the allegation, while no-crimes recorded within the month were included in the present study. .However, during the period of their research, Lloyd and Walmsley[27] (1989) found that the average no-criming rate during the second quarter of 1985 was 45 per cent[28].

Therefore, figures from the previous study were re-calculated on a new basis of recorded crimes:

335 cases initially recorded as rape including 25 per cent no-crimes;

464 cases initially recorded as rape including 45 per cent no-crimes.

Using the base figure of 464, calculations in the previous study give the following:

45 per cent no-crimed;

10 per cent NFA-ed;

7 per cent undetected;

2 per cent cautioned;

35 per cent reached court;

7 per cent found not guilty/discharged at court;

27 per cent resulted in some conviction at court, 19 per cent of these for rape.

---

27   This figure was an estimate based on the 1985 data also used in the previous rape study (Grace et al, 1992). See appendix A for more information on the bases on which the two rape studies are compared.

28   Although there was considerable variation between forces (0 to 86 per cent).

Appendix C

Crimed cases

Table C.1:   **Relationship between complainant and suspect-reported rapes**

	per cent	(n)
Stranger	**11**	**(38)**
Acquaintances	**39**	**(135)**
Met within 24 hours		(66)
Met more than 24 hours before		(47)
Known vaguely		(14)
Prostitute and client		(7)
Intimates	**50**	**(171)**
Relative (not father)		(5)
Parental figure		(27)
Current husband		(18)
Former husband		(6)
Current cohabitee		(2)
Former cohabitee		(1)
Current boyfriend		(33)
Former boyfriend		(39)
Work colleague		(3)
Friend		(29)
Family friend		(8)
TOTAL (n)	100	(344)

Note: n=344 of 360 crimed rapes for which relationship is known

Table C.2:   Marital status of complainant

	Stranger %	Acquaintance %	Intimate %	All %
Single	55	73	60	65
Cohabiting/long-term relationship	24	12	19	17
Married	10	8	9	9
Separated	7	3	8	6
Divorced	3	5	3	4
Widowed	-	-	1	<1
TOTAL (n)	100 (29)	100 (121)	100 (163)	100 (321)

Notes:
1.   n=321 of 360 crimed rapes for which complainant's marital status and relationship were known.
2.   Percentages do not always add up to 100 due to rounding.

Table C.3:   Age of complainant by complainant/suspect relationship

Age	Stranger %	Acquaintance %	Intimate %	Total % (n)
Under 12	-	32	68	100 (31)
13-15	10	52	38	100 (69)
16-25	13	41	46	100 (124)
26-35	14	27	59	100 (71)
36-45	4	44	52	100 (27)
Over 45	22	22	56	100 (18)
TOTAL (n)	11	39	50	100 (353)

Notes:
1.   n=353 of 360 crimed rapes for which age of complainant and complainant/suspect relationship were known.
2.   Percentages do not always add up to 100 due to rounding.

Circumstances surrounding the attack

Consensual contact

Table C.4: Degree of consensual contact prior to rape

	Stranger %	Acquaintance %	Intimate %	All %
Had sexual intercourse with suspect	-	2	4	3
Had sexual contact (not intercourse)	-	2	3	2
Had prior sexual relationship with suspect	-	1	49	25
Voluntarily kissed with suspect	-	11	5	7
Allowed suspect to put his arm round her	-	3	1	2
Accepted invitation into suspect's house	-	16	4	8
Accepted a lift with suspect	-	11	2	5
Walked home with suspect	-	6	1	3
Danced with suspect	-	5	-	2
Case of child abuse	-	-	17	9
Other	-	31	11	18
No consensual contact immediately prior to attack	100	14	4[29]	18
TOTAL (n)	100 (36)	100 (126)	100 (167)	100 (332)

Notes:
1. n=332 of 360 crimed rapes for which consensual contact and relationship were known.
2. Percentages do not always add up to 100 due to rounding
3. 'Other' covers a range of circumstances: for example, where the complainant woke up in the suspect's bed, she gave him directions or he showed her round a house.

---

[29] Consensual contact was the degree of contact immediately prior to the attack and therefore was recorded as none if, for instance, a complainant woke to the suspect in her bedroom, which might involve intimates.

Location of attack

Table C.5:   Location of first offence

	Stranger %	Acquaintance %	Intimate %	All %
Workplace	-	-	1	<1
Home of victim	5	15	34	23
Home of suspect	-	27	22	22
Home of complainant and suspect	-	1	32	16
Other indoor/private place	16	24	5	14
Park/green site in town or built up area	16	4	1	4
Field/countryside	-	-	-	-
Suspect's car	3	10	2	5
Complainant's car	-	-	1	<1
Public area	51	16	2	13
Waste ground	5	2	-	1
Other	3	2	1	1
TOTAL (n)	100 (37)	100 (135)	100 (168)	100 (344)

Notes:
1. n=344 crimed rapes for which location of attack and relationship were known.
2. Percentages do not always add up to 100 due to rounding.
3. Including alleyway, street area, railway station, bus stop.
4. Including building sites, rubbish dumps, disused areas of land.

Violence

Table C.6:   Use of violence

	Stranger %	Acquaintance %	Intimate %	All %
Some violence	74	59	59	61
No violence	3	22	21	20
No information	23	19	20	19
TOTAL	100 (38)	100 (135)	100 (171)	100 (344)

Notes:
1. n=344 crimed rapes for which use of violence and relationship were known.
2. Percentages do not always add up to 100 due to rounding

Defence

Table C.7: Main defence used

	Stranger %	Acquaintance %	Intimate %	All %
Total denial of offence	8	6	11	9
Issue of consent	8	23	16	18
Disputed circumstances		4	2	3
None specified	5	4	4	3
No information	79	63	67	67
TOTAL (n)	100 (38)	100 (135)	100 (171)	100 (344)

Notes:
1. n=344 crimed rapes for which main defence used and relationship were known.
2. Percentages do not always add up to 100 due to rounding.

Table C.8: Defence used related to use of violence

	Some violence %	No violence %	No information %	All (n)
Total denial of offence	8	9	10	(8)
Issue of consent	22	15	6	(17)
Disputed circumstances	3	3	1	(3)
None specified	5	4	-	(4)
No information	62	69	83	(68)
TOTAL (n)	100 (211)	100 (68)	100 (81)	100 (360)

Notes:
1. n= 360 crimed rapes for which main defence used and use of violence were known.
2. Percentages do not always add up to 100 due to rounding

Table C.9: Age of complainant and degree of violence

	Under 12	13-15	16-25	26-35	36-45	Over 45	All
Some violence	16	47	72	65	55	67	60
No violence	29	26	12	17	19	33	19
No information	55	27	16	18	26	-	21
TOTAL (n)	100 (31)	100 (73)	100 (129)	100 (71)	100 (31)	100 (18)	100 (353)

Notes:
1. n=353 initially recorded rapes for which defendant age and use of violence were known.
2. Percentages do not always add up to 100 due to rounding

Appendix D

Multivariate analyses

Table D.1: **Logistic regression analysis predicting no-crime decisions by the police**

Variable	B	Standard Error	Wald Statistic	Signif	R	Exp (B)
Age of complainant (Under 16)			12.2242	.0067	.1064	
16-25 years	.8089	.2992	7.3077	.0069	.0982	2.2454
26-35 year	.9816	.3309	8.8019	.0030	.1112	2.6686
Over 35 years	1.0442	.3523	8.7841	.0030	.1110	2.8411
Use of violence	-1.3512	.2314	34.1059	.0000	.2416	.2589
Constant	-1.1461	.2341	23.9674	.0000		

Notes:
1. n=483 (complainants and suspects). Data were missing in seven cases.
2. Other variables tested were relationship, marital status, place of contact, location of attack, threat of violence, injury and time of complaint.

Table D.2: **Logistic regression analysis predicting no further action decisions by the police**

Variable	B	Standard Error	Wald Statistic	Signif	R	Exp (B)
Age of complainant (Under 16)			45.8975	.0000	.3199	
16-25 years	1.7448	.3702	22.2136	.0000	.2277	5.7246
26-35 years	2.8783	.4593	39.2712	.0000	.3092	17.7840
Over 35 years	2.4319	.4785	25.8348	.0000	.2473	11.3806
Use of violence	-1.2507	.3172	15.5481	.0001	-.1864	.2863
Consensual contact	1.3171	.4461	8.7187	.0031	.1313	3.7325
Constant	-2.0620	.5130	16.1544	.0001		

Notes:
1. n=282 (complainants and suspects). Data were missing in 30 cases.
2. Other variables tested were relationship, marital status, place of contact, location of attack, threat of violence, injury and time of complaint

Logistic regression identifies which factors are independently associated with a particular outcome variable when all other factors are held constant. However, it should be borne in mind that any significant statistical relationship between variables does not necessarily imply a causal relationship between the two. A range of variables[32] were tested to explore their association with police decisions to no-crime cases and to take no further action. Numbers were too small to produce significant associations at the CPS and court stages.

---

32   The independent variables selected were age of complainant, relationship between complainant and suspect, degree of consensual contact, place of initial contact, location of offence, use of violence and extent of injury.

In order to predict no-criming and no further action being taken by the police, the most satisfactory model was constructed using the following variables: age of complainant and use of violence, as well as evidence of consensual contact in the case of NFA.

The estimated coefficients (B) produced by the model are shown in Tables C.1 and C.2. Each coefficient represents a change in the 'log odds' of no-criming or no further action (i.e. a change in the likelihood of these disposals) associated with a one-unit increase in a predictor variable, while controlling for all other predictor variables. It can be seen that for all predictor variables an increase in value is associated with a greater likelihood in a case being no-crimed or NFA-ed.

Because the size of the predictor variables will affect the size coefficient estimate, to obtain a comparable indicator of the effect of the different predictor variables, it is necessary also to look at the Wald statistic and the R statistic. The latter can range in value from -1 to +1 (a positive value indicating that as the variable increases, so does the chances of a case being no-crimed or NFA-ed, while a negative value indicates the opposite), and is a measure of the relative (and partial) contribution of each variable to the model.

In the final models used, violence and age were found to predict no-criming decisions and violence, age and consensual contact were found to predict the police taking no further action.

Appendix E

Research on the experiences of rape complainants

An issue emerging from this study as worthy of further research is that of complainants' experiences of the criminal justice system. Complainant withdrawals account for the majority of the attrition rate of rape cases and it is necessary to investigate further why this is happening. Findings from the present research are limited since just four women agreed to be interviewed. In fact, there is a dearth of research on this subject. However, some of the relevant work that has been carried out is summarised below.

Adler, 1990

This was a postal survey to discover how women who reported rape or a serious sexual assault to the Metropolitan Police and whose cases had been crimed viewed their treatment by the police; 103 women reporting between May 1990 and February 1991 responded. It was found that 89 per cent of respondents were satisfied or very satisfied with their treatment by women police officers and 76 per cent were satisfied or very satisfied with the male detective investigating the case. Adler concluded, "Attitudes to victims of rape in the Met are now overwhelmingly caring and sympathetic. The vast majority of women speak very favourably indeed of their experience of reporting". (Adler, 1991, p.1115).

Lees and Gregory, 1993

This study was concerned mainly with attrition rates in sexual assault cases. 24 women were interviewed who had reported sexual assault in North London between 1988 and 1990. Only four had been involved in cases of rape or attempted rape. They found that 75 per cent of the women were generally satisfied with their treatment by the police. Several complainants, however, were not satisfied with their treatment and few were told of the outcome of their cases. The authors concluded, "The service provided by the police has greatly improved. The police are to be congratulated for these improvements". (Lees and Gregory, 1993, p.23).

Temkin, 1997

This study cast a shadow of doubt on any optimistic assumptions about new police regimes; 23 women who reported rape to the Sussex police between 1991 and 1993 were interviewed in depth. Overall, the majority of women (57 per cent) were fairly positive about the service provided by the police, while 43 per cent expressed more negative views. One conclusion drawn in this study was that, "Old police practices and attitudes, widely assumed to have been vanished, are still in evidence and continue to cause victims pain and trauma". (Temkin, 1997, p.527)

Temkin, 1999

Seventeen women whose cases were recorded as rape between 1993 and 1995 were interviewed in depth about their overall attitudes and experiences of police processes, from reporting to the trial; 21 police officers were also interviewed, eight having been involved in cases in the victims sample. The study findings indicate that although police guidelines provide a framework for a system of care for victims, in practice they are not always followed. Indeed, disbelieving and stereotypical attitudes persist about women who report rape .

It is worth bearing in mind that women who were included in these research projects were those who responded to questionnaires or letters, who might have had different experiences from those who did not respond.

Bibliography and references

Alder, Z. (1987). *Rape on trial.* London: Routledge and Kegan Paul.

Adler, Z. (1991). 'Picking up the pieces'. *Police Review* (1991), May, 1114.

Chambers, G. and Millar, A. (1986). *Prosecuting sexual assault.* Edinburgh: HMSO (A Scottish Office social research study).

Criminal Justice and Public Order Act 1994.

Davis, G. and Westcott, H. (1992). "Video-technology and the child witness" in (Eds) Dent, H. and Flin, R. *Children as witnesses.* Chichester: John Wiley and Sons

Grace, S., Lloyd, C. and Smith, L. J. F. (1992). *Rape: from recording to conviction.* Research and Planning Unit Paper No.71.

Holmstrom, L. and Burgess, A. (1978). *The victim of rape: institutional reactions.* Wiley-interscience.

Home Office Circular 69/1986.

Hough, M. (1995). *Anxiety about crime: findings from the 1994 British Crime Survey,* Home Office Research Study No.147. London HMSO.

Langan, P.A. and Farrington, D.P. (1998). *Crime and Justice in the United States and in England and Wales, 1981-96,* US Department of Justice, Bureau of Justice Statistics.

Lees, S. and Gregory, J. (1993). *Rape and sexual assault: a study of attrition.* Islington Council.

Lees, S. and Gregory, J. (1996). 'Attrition in rape and sexual assault cases', *British Journal of Criminology*, vol 36, no.1, pp 1-17.

Lloyd, C. and Walmsley, R. (1989). *Changes in rape offences and sentencing.* Home Office Research Study No.105. London: HMSO.

Quinsey, V. L. and Upfold, D. (1985). "Rape completion and victim injury as a function of female resistance strategy". *Canadian Journal of Behavioural Science,* Vol 17, No.1.

Sex Offences (Amendment) Act 1976.

Soothill, K. and Grover, C. (1998). 'The public portrayal of rape sentencing: what the public learns of rape sentencing from newspapers', *Criminal Law Review,* 1998, pp455-464.

Stanko, E. (1990). *Everyday violence,* London: Pandora Press.

Temkin, J. (1987). *Rape and the legal process.* London: Sweet and Maxwell.

Temkin, J. (1997). 'Plus ca change: reporting rape in the 1990s', *British Journal of Criminology,* vol37, no.4, pp507-28.

Temkin, J. (1999). 'Reporting rape in London: a qualitative study', *Howard Journal of Criminal Justice,* February 1999.

Victim Support publication (1996). *Women, Rape and the Criminal Justice System,* Victim Support.

Wright, R. (1984). 'A note of the attrition of rape cases', *British Journal of Criminology,* vol.24, no.4, pp339-400.

Publications

List of research publications

The most recent research reports published are listed below. A **full** list of publications is available on request from the Research, Development and Statistics Directorate, Information and Publications Group.

Home Office Research Studies (HORS)

186. **The restricted hospital order: from court to the community.** Robert Street. 1998.

187. **Reducing Offending: An assessment of research evidence on ways of dealing with offending behaviour.** Edited by Peter Goldblatt and Chris Lewis. 1998.

188. **Lay visiting to police stations.** Mollie Weatheritt and Carole Vieira. 1998

189. **Mandatory drug testing in prisons: The relationship between MDT and the level and nature of drug misuse.** Kimmett Edgar and Ian O'Donnell. 1998

190. **Trespass and protest: policing under the Criminal Justice and Public Order Act 1994.** Tom Bucke and Zoë James. 1998.

191. **Domestic Violence: Findings from a new British Crime Survey self-completion questionnaire.** Catriona Mirrlees-Black. 1999.

192. **Explaining reconviction following a community sentence: the role of social factors.** Chris May. 1999.

193. **Domestic Violence Matters: an evaluation of a development project.** Liz Kelly. 1999.

194. **Increasing confidence in community sentences: the results of two demonstration projects.** Carol Hedderman, Tom Ellis and Darren Sugg. 1999

Research Findings

63. **Neighbourhood watch co-ordinators.** Elizabeth Turner and Banos Alexandrou. 1997.

64. **Attitudes to punishment: findings from the 1996 British Crime Survey.** Michael Hough and Julian Roberts. 1998.

65. **The effects of video violence on young offenders.** Kevin Browne and Amanda Pennell. 1998.

66. **Electronic monitoring of curfew orders: the second year of the trials.** Ed Mortimer and Chris May. 1998.

67. **Public perceptions of drug-related crime in 1997.** Nigel Charles. 1998.

68. **Witness care in magistrates' courts and the youth court.** Joyce Plotnikoff and Richard Woolfson. 1998.

69. **Handling stolen goods and theft: a market reduction approach.** Mike Sutton. 1998.

70. **Drug testing arrestees.** Trevor Bennett. 1998.

71. **Prevention of plastic card fraud.** Michael Levi and Jim Handley. 1998.

72. **Offending on bail and police use of conditional bail.** David Brown. 1998.

73. **Voluntary after-care.** Mike Maguire, Peter Raynor, Maurice Vanstone and Jocelyn Kynch. 1998.

74. **Fast-tracking of persistent young offenders.** John Graham. 1998.

75. **Mandatory drug testing in prisons – an evaluation.** Kimmett Edgar and Ian O'Donnell. 1998.

76. **The prison population in 1997: a statistical review.** Philip White. 1998.

77. **Rural areas and crime: findings from the British crime survey.** Catriona Mirrlees-Black. 1998.

78. **A review of classification systems for sex offenders.** Dawn Fisher and George Mair. 1998.

79. **An evaluation of the prison sex offender treatment programme.** Anthony Beech et al. 1998.

80. **Age limits for babies in prison: some lessons from abroad.** Diane Caddle. 1998.

81. **Motor projects in England & Wales: an evaluation.** Darren Sugg. 1998

82. **HIV/Aids risk behaviour among adult male prisoners.** John Strange et al. 1998.

83. **Concern about crime: findings from the 1998 British Crime Survey.** Catriona Mirrlees-Black and Jonathan Allen. 1998.

84. **Transfers from prison to hospital - the operation of section 48 of the Mental Health Act 1983.** Ronnie Mackay and David Machin. 1998.

85. **Evolving crack cocaine careers.** Kevin Brain, Howard Parker and Tim Bottomley. 1998.

86. **Domestic Violence: Findings from the BCS self-completion questionnaire.** 1999. Catriona Mirrlees-Black and Carole Byron. 1999.

87. **Incentives and earned privileges for prisoners – an evaluation.** Alison Liebling, Grant Muir, Gerry Rose and Anthony Bottoms. 1999.

88. **World Prison Population List.** Roy Walmsley. 1999.

89. **Probation employment schemes in inner London and Surrey – an evaluation.** Chris Samo, Michael Hough, Claire Nee and Victoria Herrington. 1999.

90. **Reconviction of offenders sentenced or released from prison in 1994.** Chris Kershaw. 1999.

91. **Domestic violence matters: an evaluation of a development project.** Liz Kelly. 1999.

92. **Increasing confidence in community sentences.** Carol Hedderman, Tom Ellis and Darren Sugg. 1999.

Occasional Papers

Evaluation of a Home Office initiative to help offenders into employment. Ken Roberts, Alana Barton, Julian Buchanan and Barry Goldson. 1997.

The impact of the national lottery on the horse-race betting levy. Simon Field and James Dunmore. 1997.

The cost of fires. A review of the information available. Donald Roy. 1997.

Monitoring and evaluation of WOLDS remand prison and comparisons with public-sector prisons, in particular HMP Woodhill. A Keith Bottomley, Adrian James, Emma Clare and Alison Liebling. 1997.

Evaluation of the 'One Stop Shop' and victim statement pilot projects. Carolyn Hoyle, Ed Cape, Rod Morgan and Andrew Sanders. 1998.

Restorative Justice: an overview. Tony Marshall. 1999.

Step 3: an evaluation of the prison sex offender treatment programme. Anthony Beech, Dawn Fisher and Richard Beckett. 1999.

Requests for Publications

Home Office Research Studies, Research Findings and *Occasional Papers* can be requested from:

Research, Development and Statistics Directorate
Information and Publications Group
Room 201, Home Office
50 Queen Anne's Gate
London SW1H 9AT
Telephone: 0171-273 2084
Facsimile: 0171-222 0211
Internet: http://www.homeoffice.gov.uk/rds/index.htm
E-mail: rds.ho@gtnet.gov.uk